After the Story's Over

Your Enrichment Guide to 88 Read-Aloud Children's Classics

Linda K. Garrity

Illustrated by Jackie Moore

Scott, Foresman and Company
Glenview, Illinois   London

 **Good Year Books**

are available for preschool through grade 6 and for every basic curriculum subject plus many enrichment areas. For more Good Year Books, contact your local bookseller or educational dealer. For a complete catalog with information about other Good Year Books, please write:

> Good Year Books
> Scott, Foresman and Company
> 1900 East Lake Avenue
> Glenview, Illinois 60025

6 EBI 95 94 93

ISBN 0-673-38836-0

Contents

Contents by Subject

Lists of Recipes

Alphabetical List

Following is a list of recipes arranged alphabetically, with the story in which each recipe is found given in parentheses.

Animal Snackers (*Bread and Jam for Frances*)

Bat Wing Brownies (*Arthur's Halloween*)

Bread and Jam Roll-Ups (*Bread and Jam for Frances*)

Cloudy with a Chance of Fruitballs (*Cloudy with a Chance of Meatballs*)

Cobweb Christmas Trees (*The Cobweb Christmas*)

Cornbread (*Ox-Cart Man*)

Cranberry Thanksgiving Bread (*Cranberry Thanksgiving*)

Dinosaur Clay (*Patrick's Dinosaurs*)

Dracula Frosting (*Arthur's Halloween*)

Grandma's Jumbo Chocolate Chip Cookies (*The Doorbell Rang*)

Granny's Humbug Carrot Bars (*Humbug Rabbit*)

Granny's Humbug Icing (*Humbug Rabbit*)

Gregory's Necklace (*Gregory, the Terrible Eater*)

Harriet's Halloween Cheese Balls (*Harriet's Halloween Candy*)

Homemade Butter (*Ox-Cart Man*)

Irish Soda Bread (*Leprechauns Never Lie*)

Jumbo Jack-O'-Lantern Cookies (*Arthur's Halloween*)

Lovely, Light, Luscious, Delectable Cake (*The Duchess Bakes a Cake*)

Lyle, Lyle Crocodiles (*The House on East 88th Street*)

Max's Boats (*Where the Wild Things Are*)

Miniature Graham Cracker Crusts (*Thanksgiving at the Tappletons'*)

Sugar Egg with Scene (*The Country Bunny and the Little Gold Shoes*)

Royal Buttercream Frosting (*The Duchess Bakes a Cake*)

Tappletons' Pumpkin Mini-Pies (*Thanksgiving at the Tappletons'*)

Trick-or-Treat Punch (*Arthur's Halloween*)

Unbirthday Cake (*A Birthday for Frances*)

Unbirthday Icing (*A Birthday for Frances*)

Unbirthday Punch (*A Birthday for Frances*)

Vampire Blood Punch (*Arthur's Halloween*)

Story List

Following is a list of recipes arranged under the story in which the recipe is found.

Arthur's Halloween
  Bat Wing Brownies
  Dracula Frosting
  Jumbo Jack-O'-Lantern Cookies
  Trick-or-Treat Punch
  Vampire Blood Punch

Birthday for Frances, A
  Unbirthday Cake
  Unbirthday Icing
  Unbirthday Punch

Bread and Jam for Frances
  Animal Snackers
  Bread and Jam Roll-Ups

Cloudy with a Chance of Meatballs
  Cloudy with a Chance of Fruitballs

Cobweb Christmas, The
  Cobweb Christmas Trees

Country Bunny and the Little Gold Shoes, The
  Sugar Egg with Scene

Cranberry Thanksgiving
  Cranberry Thanksgiving Bread

Doorbell Rang, The
  Grandma's Jumbo Chocolate Chip Cookies

Duchess Bakes a Cake, The
  Lovely, Light, Luscious, Delectable Cake
  Royal Buttercream Frosting

Gregory, the Terrible Eater
  Gregory's Necklace

Harriet's Halloween Candy
  Harriet's Halloween Cheese Balls

House on East 88th Street, The
  Lyle, Lyle Crocodiles

Humbug Rabbit
  Granny's Humbug Carrot Bars
  Granny's Humbug Icing

Leprechauns Never Lie
  Irish Soda Bread

Ox-Cart Man
  Cornbread
  Homemade Butter

Patrick's Dinosaurs
  Dinosaur Clay

Suggested Ages

Following is a list of the stories arranged according to the ages for which each story is best suited.

5–6 Baby Sister for Frances, A
Bedtime for Frances
Berenstain Bears Go to School, The
Birthday for Frances, A
Corduroy
Harry and the Terrible Whatzit
Little Engine That Could, The
My Teacher Sleeps in School
Peter's Chair
Pocket for Corduroy, A
Rabbit for Easter, A
Runaway Bunny, The
Tale of Peter Rabbit, The
There's a Nightmare in My Closet
Where the Wild Things Are

5–7 Annie and the Wild Animals
Arthur's Tooth
Arthur's Valentine
Biggest House in the World, The
Bread and Jam for Frances
Doorbell Rang, The
Gregory, the Terrible Eater
Harriet's Halloween Candy
House on East 88th Street, The
Humbug Rabbit
Little House, The
Little Rabbit's Loose Tooth
Patrick's Dinosaurs
Sometimes It's Turkey—Sometimes It's Feathers
Sweet Touch, The
Sylvester and the Magic Pebble
William's Doll

5–8 Alexander and the Terrible, Horrible, No Good, Very Bad Day
Bah! Humbug?
Cloudy with a Chance of Meatballs
Country Bunny and the Little Gold Shoes, The
Cranberry Thanksgiving
Ghost-Eye Tree, The
Ira Sleeps Over
Leo the Late Bloomer
Miss Nelson Is Missing!
Oh, Were They Ever Happy!

Introduction

Reading to children is fun! Generations of parents, teachers, and librarians have always believed in it. And today's educators increasingly support reading to children. Numerous studies have validated the importance of reading aloud to children to help them develop better reading, writing, listening, and higher-level thinking skills. The National Institute of Education in their landmark study, *Becoming a Nation of Readers*, states, "The single most important activity for building the knowledge required for eventual success in reading is reading aloud to children."[1] The study continues, "There is no substitute for a teacher who reads children good stories. It whets the appetite of children for reading, and provides a model of skillful oral reading. It is a practice that should continue throughout the grades."[2]

Merely reading a book to a child or a group of children is valuable in itself; it can become even more advantageous for youngsters if you discuss the story with them, focusing especially on the theme or central idea. This activity can evolve further into different kinds of writing or perhaps role-play. Or you might tie in some poetry for greater appreciation. Some children will enjoy and remember a story better if they can paint or draw or make something reflecting the story's theme or characters. If you have the facilities and patience, then try cooking.

All of these suggestions can involve a great deal of thought and preparation. This guidebook is designed to reduce some of that preparatory work and allow you the time to share literature with your five- to nine-year-old charges.

Format of Book Units

The format of each book unit is designed to provide a wide range of options in an easy-to-use layout. And what a wonderful world of books from which to choose, most available in inexpensive paper bindings! The bibliographic information at the beginning of each unit can assist you in requesting a book from a library or in ordering it. (The abbreviation *HB* indicates a hard binding, *LB* a library binding, and *PB* a paper binding.) The suggested ages give a rough idea of which group of youngsters will most enjoy and understand the book. Topics allow you to tie several books together for a thematic unit (check the index for this information also). The succinctly worded theme expresses the message of the book, which may help you guide the discussion.

Setting the Stage

The first part of each book presentation, Setting the Stage, is based on Madeline Hunter's and Bernice McCarthy's teaching models. It provides brief, provocative questions designed to create enthusiasm and motivation in children by reaching into their own personal experiences. During this segment of the storytelling session, the book should be face down in your lap or in some other place out of sight, so that the emphasis is on the children's experiences and reactions, not on the upcoming story.

[1]*Becoming a Nation of Readers: The Report of the Commission on Reading* (National Institute of Education, 1984), page 23.
[2]Ibid. page 51.

The Bridge

For step two, the Bridge, you should pick up the book and hold it so the cover is easily visible to the children. In this step you try to "bridge" or draw a correlation between what the children already know or have experienced and talked about, and what they can expect to hear in the story. By carefully asking a question or two, but not revealing too much about the story, you can build a sense of curiosity in the children as well as direct their listening toward the story's main idea.

Presentation of the Book

Once the children are primed for the presentation, you can begin reading. Hold the book so that its cover faces the children (or hold or sit next to a single child); the illustrations are an integral part of the storytelling experience. Choose an oral technique that is comfortable for you. Probably the key factor is reading books that you yourself truly enjoy. Children will quickly pick up on your feelings and will tend to associate certain books with the adult who first presented the stories.

Discussion Questions

After reading the story, go directly to the Discussion Questions. These questions are designed to help children discover the theme of the book and also to identify with some aspect of the story. Limit the number of questions to those that seem most intriguing to you and most applicable to your child or group of children. Ideally, children should be able to answer the questions raised in the Bridge section. This process reinforces a meaningful comprehension pattern:
  1. Identifying what we need to know to understand content
  2. Describing what we need and/or want to learn from content
  3. Processing (reading or listening) of content
  4. Discussing what we learned from content

Questioning Model

The questioning model (see Table 1) encourages both convergent and divergent thinking and aims toward higher-level mental processing; the divergent questions (left-brained) require more creativity and imagination. Although the model is influenced by Benjamin Bloom's work, it is designed specifically for literary study. The questions do not follow a hierarchy, nor are all categories used in each story. Simpler stories have more questions in the convergent categories, while more complex books lend themselves to more divergent questioning. Be selective in choosing questions. Although too many questions can ruin a story, eliminating them altogether fails to allow the opportunity to share the literary experience.

  Developing quality questions is not that difficult. The challenge lies in gleaning higher-level answers from the children. Some suggestions for creating the atmosphere and attitudes for meaningful discussions follow:
  1. Model the levels of answers. This step is the most important. Start your program by asking questions and then answering many of them. Offer a variety of answers expressing widely divergent opinions. Always offer explanations for each particular answer or opinion. This procedure will effectively display the divergency and reasoning you are seeking.

Table 1

Category	Convergent Thinking			Divergent Thinking		
	Significant Detail	Logical Deduction	Main Idea	Personal Relevance	Personal Prophecy	Personal Judgment
Definition	Literal fact found verbatim in the text, necessary to understanding primary or secondary themes	Conclusion or opinion based in part upon the text and in part upon the background and logical thinking of the reader	Primary theme plus secondary themes, if present	Correlation between experiences or feelings of characters in the text and similar experiences and feelings of the reader	Creative speculation about the characters, plot, or theme	Value judgment, comparing the theme or events to the reader's personal value system or to themes of similar selections
Questions	What facts do you need to know to understand the theme or themes?	What ideas or events are important to the story?	What is the overall message of the selection? It can be helpful to start with main idea questions.	What similar experiences or feelings does the reader have to events or feelings of characters in the text? These questions help personalize literature for the reader.	"What if" questions concerning plot, characterization, and point of view	Do you personally agree with the theme of the story or the beliefs of the characters? Or, what other pieces of literature use a similar theme or charactization?
Answers	These answers can be recited from memory or copied from a text. Remember, a detail is significant only if it has a direct bearing on other ideas being explored in text.	These answers should require a knowledge of the text as well as some reasoning based on the reader's background.	These answers should demonstrate that the reader understands the primary and secondary themes of the text ; however, the theme is often revealed subtly in other types of questions.	These answers require knowledge of the text coupled with a personal revelation.	The answers, of course, vary with the individual, though the subtle implication is that the various elements of the story are critical for the development of the theme.	These answers have the reader compare a theme or idea from the text to his/her own value system, or possibly to the theme of a different selection (books, poetry, movies).

2. Provide meaningful pauses. Enforce a brief thinking period between the question and the acceptance of answers. Remember that introspection, not speed, is the goal.
3. Encourage contributions. Reply to answers with warmth and respect so that children realize their contributions are accepted and appreciated, while still leaving the questioning process open to new and divergent views.
4. Indicate divergency. Preface questions higher than the significant detail level with a key phrase that indicates divergent answers are being sought, for example, "In your opinion . . ." or "What do you think . . . ."
5. Use body language and physical arrangement. An adult's direct eye contact, friendly smile, and gently nodding head can go a long way toward encouraging a shy child to express an opinion. Provide a setting conducive to a mood of dinner table discussion—courteous of others' opinions but warm enough to create spontaneity. Sometimes, semicircular seating arrangements or floor seating provides a more relaxed atmosphere.
6. Work all the crowd. Use a type of questioning aimed at a wide range of children, especially the learning-disabled, who often possess a wealth of background information to share, and gifted children, who enjoy the challenge of creative thinking.
7. Reveal personal anecdotes and feelings. Although you should avoid value judgments, take advantage of opportunities to reveal your childhood fears of the dark or stories of how you lost your first tooth. When you show that you are not reticent about making a personal correlation between your life's experiences and literature, your children will be more apt to do the same.

Enrichment Activities

The enrichment activities are designed to offer creative extension to the stories. The illustrator, Jackie Moore, has used her background as both a classroom teacher and an art teacher to develop age-appropriate art activities that are practical, yet unique. Child-oriented recipes make classroom-sized amounts (25–30 portions). Writing activities provide children with a wide range of projects for written expression. The poetry selections were all drawn from the following highly popular anthologies:

Prelutsky, Jack (1984). *The New Kid on the Block*. New York: Greenwillow Books.
Prelutsky, Jack (1983). *The Random House Book of Poetry for Children*. New York: Random House.
Silverstein, Shel (1981). *A Light in the Attic*. New York: Harper and Row.
Silverstein, Shel (1974). *Where the Sidewalk Ends*. New York: Harper and Row.

Pointers throughout the book try to provide guidance that will help you make the activities as successful as possible.

Reading to children *is* fun. And "after the story's over," the fun can go on—for both you and your children!

Book Unit Activities

Alexander and the Terrible, Horrible, No Good, Very Bad Day

AUTHOR: Judith Viorst

ILLUSTRATOR: Ray Cruz

PUBLISHING INFORMATION:
Atheneum, 1972, HB, ISBN 9-689-30072-7
Aladdin, 1976, PB, ISBN 9-689-70428-3
Aladdin, 1987, PB, ISBN 9-689-71173-5

SUGGESTED AGES: 5–8

TOPICS: Friends
School
Siblings

THEMES: Everyone has an occasional bad day. Sometimes one person's bad mood can affect others.

Setting the Stage

Have you ever had a day when nothing seemed to go right? I have had plenty of days like that. Most of us would all like to forget our very worst days, but I'll tell you about a rather bad day that I had and then you might like to share a similar bad day you have had. (The adult could briefly narrate a day of humorous-type misfortunes, being careful to set a light-hearted tone. Sadly, many children have experienced bad days that are truly tragic; such days should not be handled as a class discussion.)

Bridge

The little boy, Alexander, who is on the cover of our story, does not look too happy. I wonder what happened to him on his terrible, horrible, no good, very bad day. (Pause.) Let's find out in Judith Viorst's story.

Discussion Questions

Logical Deduction:
Why didn't Mrs. Dickens like Alexander's picture of the invisible castle? (He hadn't drawn anything.)

Personal Relevance:
Being someone's best friend makes us feel happy inside. Losing that best friend makes us feel angry or sad. What can you do to make things better when you lose a best friend? What are some things that probably won't help?

Logical Deduction:
(Show the page picturing the dad at the office.) What do you suppose the dad is thinking? What do you suppose the mom is thinking? (Perhaps they are thinking that bringing the children to the office was a poor idea because Alexander is messing things up.)

Personal Relevance:
Alexander hates lima beans. Most children dislike some foods. What do you do when your parent serves you something you dislike? What do you do if you are at a friend's house and are served something you dislike?

Main Idea:
Do you think Alexander would not have any more bad days if he moved to Australia? (No.) Why do you think that way? (Bad days can occur anywhere.)

Personal Prophecy:
If you had been Alexander, what would you have done to make your day better?

Activities

Poetry:
I wonder if Marchette Chute didn't have Alexander in mind when she wrote the poem "The Wrong Start," from *The Random House Book of Poetry for Children*, page 132. See if you agree.

Alexander went from being Paul's best friend to only his what? (His third best friend.) That's a big drop in friendship. Here is a puzzling poem about boys and their best friends, "Puzzle," by Arnold Spilka, from *The Random House Book of Poetry for Children*, page 104. See if you can figure it out!

(Some teachers of very young children substitute "dislike" for "hate" in this poem, since "hate" can be a troublesome word.)

Alexander wasn't the only person to draw an invisible picture. Look at the picture on this page as I read the poem by Shel Silverstein entitled "Invisible Boy," from *Where the Sidewalk Ends*, page 82. (Children could then take a few moments to study and "draw" an invisible picture, and then take turns to show the class, describing the picture and colors used.)

Crafts:
The sneakers can be used to decorate a wall or hallway by cutting them out and attaching them to the surface. See Activity 1.

The undercover code ring is easy to make and fun for children to play with. Older children might like to use the number ring as a pattern to create their own code ring. Books on codes and secret writing can provide additional ideas for them. See Activity 2.

Drama:
Small groups of children could act out each of the scenes in the story. After a short preparation period, each group could present a skit for the class.

Directions:

Alexander got stuck with plain white sneakers. Design a super-special pair for him.

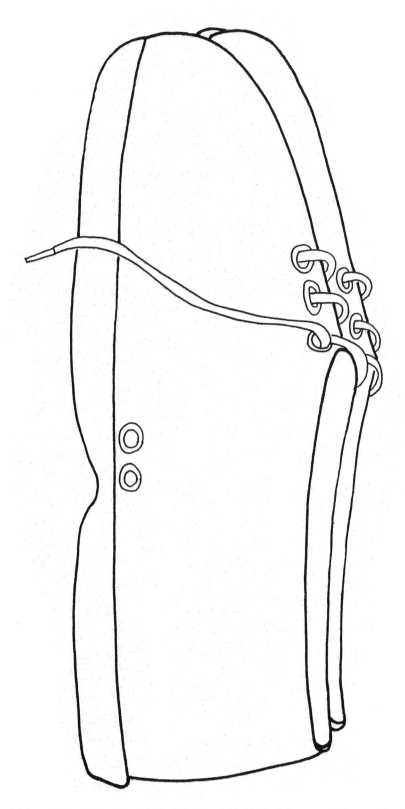

Directions:

Alexander found only cereal in his breakfast cereal box, while Nick found a Junior Undercover Agent Code Ring. Follow the directions to make an enlargement of Nick's ring.

1. Cut out the ring.

2. Put a brass fastener through both center dots.

3. Turn the number circle to make your own code.

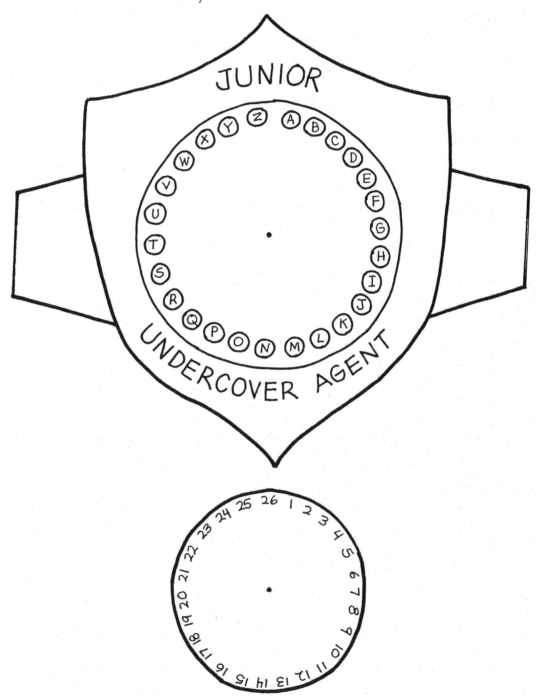

Amos and Boris

AUTHOR: William Steig

ILLUSTRATOR: William Steig

PUBLISHING INFORMATION:
Farrar, Straus, & Giroux, 1971, HB,
ISBN 0-374-30278-2
Penguin Puffin, 1971, PB, ISBN 0-14-050229–7

SUGGESTED AGES: 6–9

TOPIC: Friends

THEMES: Small can be mighty.
One good turn deserves another.

Setting the Stage

Have you ever had a good friend do something very nice for you? Were you later able to do something nice for that friend?

Bridge

On the cover of today's story we see a small mouse who both gave some help and received some help from an unusual friend. Let's listen to William Steig's story, *Amos and Boris*, to find out who the unusual friend was and how the friends helped each other.

Discussion Questions

Logical Deduction:
Why do you think "The Rodent" was a good name for Amos's boat? (All mice are rodents.)

Logical Deduction:
Amos found it hard to believe Boris was a mammal. Why would a fishlike creature like a whale be considered a mammal? (The answer can be found in an encyclopedia, as well as other books on whales, though occasionally a child may be knowledgeable on the topic. A whale is considered a mammal because its young are born alive and are fed milk from the mother's body; it has warm blood; it has lungs and must breathe air from above the water; and it has some bristly hair on its head.)

Personal Relevance:
Close your eyes and think about a good friend. Think of two reasons why you are such good friends. Now open your eyes. What are your reasons?

Logical Deduction:
Why did Boris laugh to himself at the thought of Amos helping him? (Amos was so small, and Boris was so large.)

Main Idea:
What lesson did Boris learn in the end? (Size has nothing to do with helpfulness.)

Personal Relevance:
Sometimes children are like Amos, the mouse, when it comes to helping grown-ups. When are you too small to help grown-ups? What are some things you do to help grown-ups where size doesn't matter?

Activities

Older children will enjoy hearing two well-known fables, *Androcles and the Lion* and *The Lion and the Mouse*, found in most fable anthologies. Eight- and nine-year-olds will be able to draw analogies among the morals of the three stories.

Research:
Children can use the whale pattern and lined paper to create booklets for whale studies. Using reference and science books, they can read about whales and then write down the facts they consider the most interesting. The whale booklets could then be shared with the whole group. See Activity 3.

Writing:
Use the following discussion to trigger a creative-writing activity.

The ending to this story could be called *bittersweet*. That's an unusual word. Do you have any guesses about what it might mean? What part of the ending is bitter? What part is sweet? Write a new ending to the story that is entirely sweet.

Pairs of children can write letters between the two characters. They need to "get into" the characters to make the letters believable. (The letters may be hilarious, as well as creative.)

The story of Amos and Boris can be used as a springboard to studying figures of speech. Amos liked "mousing around," and Boris liked "whaling about." Other expressions based on animals are "squirreling away nuts," "wolfing down food," "pigging out," "horsing around," "skunking up the place," and "chickening out." Ask children to think of other expressions or create new ones. Ed Gwynne's books would work in nicely here. They are as follows:

A Chocolate Moose for Dinner
The King Who Rained
A Little Pigeon Toad
The Sixteen-Hand Horse

Children could draw pictures of animal-type figures of speech, using the expressions as captions.

Drama:
The book *Amos and Boris* is ideal for pairs of children to act out. An eyebrow pencil can be used to make whiskers for the mouse and a larger mouth for the whale. Encourage children to be creative in choosing props. For example, one pair of children used a blanket for the ocean and a pillow for the boat. Allow plenty of time for the children to decide upon the scenes to be included, as well as the best combination of dialogue and pantomime. Acting out stories is great fun for the children, and at the same time it requires complete knowledge of the text.

From *After the Story's Over: Your Enrichment Guide to 88 Read-Aloud Children's Classics*, published by Scott, Foresman and Company. Copyright © 1991 Linda K. Garrity.

Name _____

Directions:

Using this pattern as the cover, make a fact book about whales. Cut
several sheets of lined paper for your book.

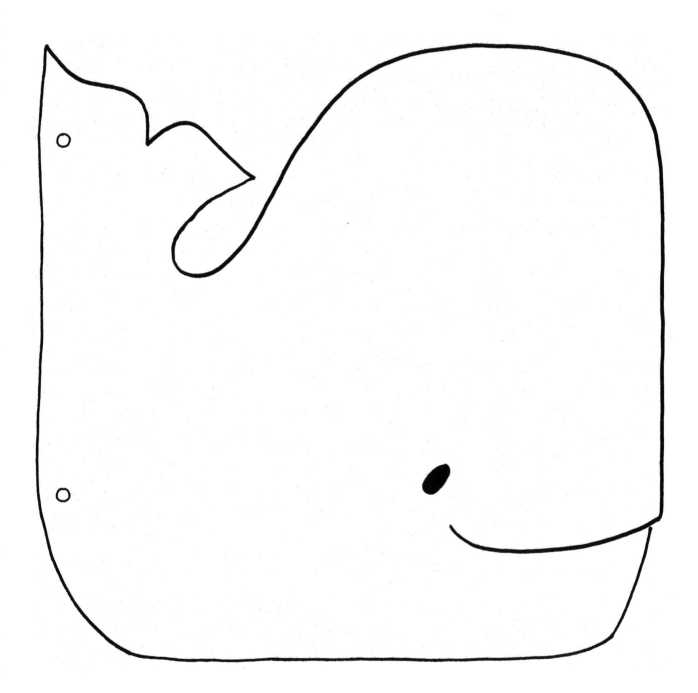

Annie and the Wild Animals

AUTHOR: Jan Brett

ILLUSTRATOR: Jan Brett

PUBLISHING INFORMATION:
Houghton Mifflin, 1985, HB,
ISBN 0-395-37800-1
Houghton Mifflin Sandpiper, 1989,
ISBN 0-395-51006-6

SUGGESTED AGES: 5–7

TOPICS: Animals
Seasons
Spring
Winter

THEME: Wild animals are not usually suitable as household pets.

Setting the Stage

Have you ever tried to tame a wild animal, like a rabbit or a chipmunk? What happened?

Bridge

The little girl on our cover, Annie, tried to tame some wild animals for pets. What do you suppose happened when she tried to tame them? Let's read this beautiful book by Jan Brett to find out. (The borders provide a running commentary of Taffy's exploits; try to allow children an opportunity to examine the book individually.)

Discussion Questions

Logical Deduction:
Why did Taffy sleep all day, eat more food, and finally disappear into the woods? (She was going to have kittens.)

Logical Deduction:
Why didn't the wild animals work out as pets? (They were too large and wild.)

Personal Prophecy:
If you had been Annie, would you have put out corncakes to get a new pet? What would you have tried?

Personal Judgment:
In most zoos people are not supposed to feed the wild animals. Why do you think zoos have that rule?

Logical Deduction:
What kinds of food would the wild animals eat in the forest, now that it was springtime? (Point out the border pictures which show some of the answers— fish, wild honey, buds on trees and bushes, plants.)

Personal Relevance:
Would you enjoy having three new little kittens as pets? Why?

Activities

Poetry:
In what season do children make snowmen? Do you think of snowmen in the summertime? Here is a poem from *Where the Sidewalk Ends*, page 65, about a very silly snowman who would like to be around in July, which is in the middle of summer!

"Snowman"

That time between winter and spring is an unusual time of year. People are always amazed at how the winter can be so cold and often snowy and then, only a few weeks later, springtime brings warmth and sunshine. The following poems, from *The Random House Book of Poetry for Children*, express those feelings about the change between winter and spring:

"Beyond Winter," by Ralph Waldo Emerson, page 38
"Smells," by Kathryn Worth, page 39
"When," by Dorothy Aldis, page 40
"The March Wind," Anonymous, page 41

Craft:
Fancy snowflakes are not too difficult for young children to do if you first teach a few children by

careful demonstration and then have them teach the others. Colored tissue paper can be very pretty in this project. A six-sided star is more difficult to create, but quite showy. See Figure 1.

Writing:

The rating scale can be an interesting activity if children are prepared beforehand. Draw a practice scale or two on the blackboard, and use animals other than those in *Annie and the Wild Animals.* Discuss the meaning of the adjectives and the significance of the three levels. Children might do the project in small groups, so they can pool their knowledge of animals. It may trigger some research for those not wanting to rely on their hunches. The illustrations in the book should help children with most of the evaluation. See Activity 4.

Figure 1 _____

To make the snowflake, you will need 9" × 9" white construction paper (or any size that is square) and melted paraffin and glitter (optional).

1. Fold the paper like this:

2. Cut off the corner points and then cut across at an angle. Cut out small shapes around the three sides and then open.

3. Dip the snowflake into the melted paraffin and sprinkle on glitter. Hang with opened paper clip or thread. These six-sided stars are very showy.

From *After the Story's Over: Your Enrichment Guide to 88 Read-Aloud Children's Classics,* published by Scott, Foresman and Company. Copyright © 1991 Linda K. Garrity.

Rating Scale for Annie's Animals

Directions:

Color in the circle to rate each of Annie's animals.

<table>
<tr><td colspan="6" align="center">Cat</td><td colspan="6"></td></tr>
<tr><td>Small</td><td>○</td><td>○</td><td>○</td><td>Large</td><td>Small</td><td>○</td><td>○</td><td>○</td><td>Large</td></tr>
<tr><td>Gentle</td><td>○</td><td>○</td><td>○</td><td>Wild</td><td>Gentle</td><td>○</td><td>○</td><td>○</td><td>Wild</td></tr>
<tr><td>Quiet</td><td>○</td><td>○</td><td>○</td><td>Loud</td><td>Quiet</td><td>○</td><td>○</td><td>○</td><td>Loud</td></tr>
<tr><td>Friendly</td><td>○</td><td>○</td><td>○</td><td>Grumpy</td><td>Friendly</td><td>○</td><td>○</td><td>○</td><td>Grumpy</td></tr>
<tr><td>Soft</td><td>○</td><td>○</td><td>○</td><td>Rough</td><td>Soft</td><td>○</td><td>○</td><td>○</td><td>Rough</td></tr>
<tr><td>Small</td><td>○</td><td>○</td><td>○</td><td>Large</td><td>Small</td><td>○</td><td>○</td><td>○</td><td>Large</td></tr>
<tr><td>Gentle</td><td>○</td><td>○</td><td>○</td><td>Wild</td><td>Gentle</td><td>○</td><td>○</td><td>○</td><td>Wild</td></tr>
<tr><td>Quiet</td><td>○</td><td>○</td><td>○</td><td>Loud</td><td>Quiet</td><td>○</td><td>○</td><td>○</td><td>Loud</td></tr>
<tr><td>Friendly</td><td>○</td><td>○</td><td>○</td><td>Grumpy</td><td>Friendly</td><td>○</td><td>○</td><td>○</td><td>Grumpy</td></tr>
<tr><td>Soft</td><td>○</td><td>○</td><td>○</td><td>Rough</td><td>Soft</td><td>○</td><td>○</td><td>○</td><td>Rough</td></tr>
<tr><td>Small</td><td>○</td><td>○</td><td>○</td><td>Large</td><td>Small</td><td>○</td><td>○</td><td>○</td><td>Large</td></tr>
<tr><td>Gentle</td><td>○</td><td>○</td><td>○</td><td>Wild</td><td>Gentle</td><td>○</td><td>○</td><td>○</td><td>Wild</td></tr>
<tr><td>Quiet</td><td>○</td><td>○</td><td>○</td><td>Loud</td><td>Quiet</td><td>○</td><td>○</td><td>○</td><td>Loud</td></tr>
<tr><td>Friendly</td><td>○</td><td>○</td><td>○</td><td>Grumpy</td><td>Friendly</td><td>○</td><td>○</td><td>○</td><td>Grumpy</td></tr>
<tr><td>Soft</td><td>○</td><td>○</td><td>○</td><td>Rough</td><td>Soft</td><td>○</td><td>○</td><td>○</td><td>Rough</td></tr>
</table>

Which animal would you like best? _____

What would you do with that animal? _____

From *After the Story's Over: Your Enrichment Guide to 88 Read-Aloud Children's Classics,* published by Scott, Foresman and Company. Copyright © 1991 Linda K. Garrity.

Arthur's Eyes*

AUTHOR: Marc Brown

ILLUSTRATOR: Marc Brown

PUBLISHING INFORMATION:
Little, Brown, 1979, HB, ISBN 0-316-11063-9
Avon Camelot, 1981, PB, ISBN 0-380-53389-8

SUGGESTED AGES: 6–8

TOPIC: New glasses

THEMES: Lack of correctional eyeglasses can cause a variety of problems.
Acquiring new glasses requires a certain amount of adjustment for children.

Setting the Stage

How many of you either wear glasses yourselves or have someone in your family who wears them? Would you tell about getting your glasses—who first thought you needed them, what was it like going to the eye doctor, and so on?

Bridge

Today we're going to hear some stories (a story) about children who needed to wear glasses (sometimes called *spectacles* or *specs*). Let's listen to how they reacted to their new glasses.

Discussion Questions

Significant Detail:
What problems did Arthur have before he got glasses? (He couldn't see well, got headaches, held the book too closely, couldn't see the blackboard so missed arithmetic problems; no one wanted him on the basketball team.)

Main Ideas:
Why did Arthur decide not to wear his glasses? (His friends made fun of him.)
    What happened to make Arthur change his mind about wearing glasses? (He mistakenly went into the girls' restroom. Later the teacher showed Arthur his own glasses, encouraging Arthur to wear his own glasses.)

Logical Deduction:
Why did the children call Arthur "four eyes"? What did that mean? (They said it to tease Arthur; "four eyes" refers to a person's two eyes plus two lenses.)

Personal Relevance:
Would it hurt your feelings if someone called you "four eyes"? Why or why not?

Activity

Craft:
The whole class can use Activity 5 to make creative eyeglasses for a spectacular Spectacles Day. A Polaroid camera would come in handy to record this event.

*See *Spectacles*, page 175, and *Watch Out, Ronald Morgan!*, page 207. (*Note:* All three stories deal with children getting new glasses. Any one of the three stories could be used alone, though the three blend together well to cover this topic.)

Directions:

Use this pattern to make your own spectacular spectacles. Cut each piece from tagboard or poster board. Add trims such as stars, hearts, or flowers.

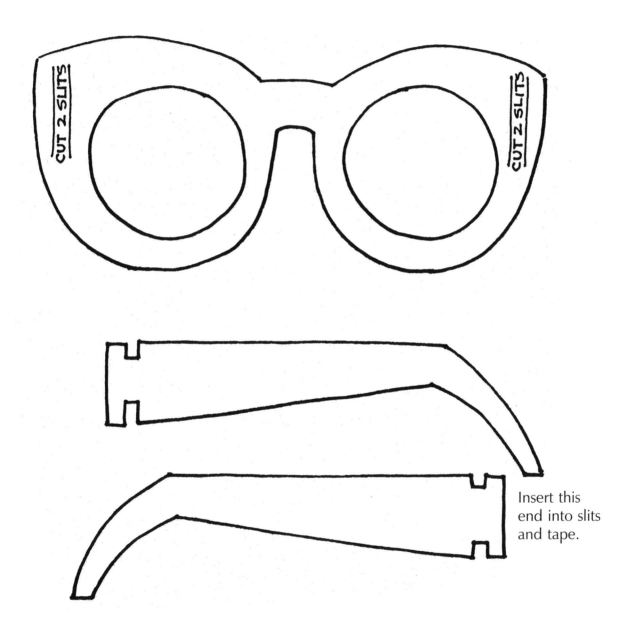

Insert this end into slits and tape.

From *After the Story's Over: Your Enrichment Guide to 88 Read-Aloud Children's Classics,* published by Scott, Foresman and Company. Copyright © 1991 Linda K. Garrity.

Arthur's Halloween

AUTHOR: Marc Brown

ILLUSTRATOR: Marc Brown

PUBLISHING INFORMATION:
Little, Brown, 1982, HB, ISBN 0-316-11116-3
Little, Brown, 1983, PB, ISBN 0-316-11059-0

SUGGESTED AGES: 6–8

TOPIC: Halloween

THEMES: Appearances can be deceiving.
Scary fun is not entertaining for everyone.

Setting the Stage

How do you get ready for Halloween? What do you usually do on Halloween night?

Bridge

Arthur is the little moose boy on the cover of our book. What is Arthur doing? Do you think he is having a good time? What do you think may have happened to cause Arthur to feel that way? Arthur *does* have a big surprise on Halloween, but it's not what we would usually think about Halloween surprises! Let's read and find out in Marc Brown's book, *Arthur's Halloween*.

Discussion Questions

Significant Detail:
How did Arthur feel about eating bat wing brownies and vampire blood punch and touching the eyeballs and brains? (He didn't want to take part; it was disgusting to him.)

Personal Judgment:
Do you think Arthur was being a big baby to refuse to take part in the Halloween party ideas or do you think the other children were mean to tease him? Why do you think that way?

Personal Prophecy:
What would you have done at the party if you had been Arthur?

Logical Deduction:
Why wouldn't the children go trick or treating to the house that gave away apples? (They prefered sweet, candy-type treats over nutritious ones.)

Personal Judgments:
What do you think are the best treats to give to children?

Do you think Buster was telling the truth when he said his brother saw someone go into the witch's house last Halloween and never come out? (Also explore the angle that the brother may have been the one to make up the story.)

Main Ideas:
What did the witch turn out to be? (She was a poor, kind, elderly widow.)

Why was her house so spooky? (It was run-down because she was poor and was physically unable to take care of it.)

Significant Detail:
What did Arthur decide to do to help Mrs. Tibble? (He decided to fix up her yard so it wouldn't look so spooky.)

Personal Prophecy:
Tell about something you and your friends could do to help someone like Mrs. Tibble.

Logical Deduction:
(This pun is amusing to children 6½–7, but younger children usually do not understand it. Since it is not pertinent to the theme of the story, the following question can be omitted for younger listeners.) At the end of the book Arthur says, "The cemetery is a great place. People are just dying to get in." What did Arthur mean? (*Dying* can mean both eager and actually dying.)

Activities

Concrete Poetry:
You can share many fine Halloween poems with children. This subject also provides a good

Figure 2 _____

opportunity for children to write their own concrete poetry. First brainstorm Halloween things (nouns). Then have children write their poems on plain paper. After they have completed the poems, they can transfer them to colored paper and cut out appropriate designs for display. (See Figure 2.)

Cooking:

When baked in a 12″ × 17″ pan, Bat-Wing Brownies make a thin, finely textured brownie that serves a crowd. Serve the punch recipes in a foil-lined, scooped-out pumpkin to impress spooky guests.

The Jumbo Jack-O'-Lantern Cookies are not very sweet and are somewhat heavy. A nutritious approach is to frost them with peanut butter and decorate with nuts and raisins. You could also frost them with Granny's Humbug Icing (cream cheese icing, page 88) and decorate them with raisins.

BAT WING BROWNIES

1. Turn on oven to 325°.
2. Mix in a large bowl with a spoon until creamy and smooth:
   1 stick margarine (take out of fridge early)
   1 cup sugar
3. Crack 4 eggs into a cup and beat with a fork. Stir into mix.
4. Add and mix:
   1 cup flour
   1 cup chocolate syrup
5. Grease a cookie sheet that has sides.
6. Pour in mix and bake for 25 minutes.

DRACULA FROSTING

1. Add to a medium mixing bowl and beat until fluffy:
   ½ cup butter or margarine
   2 cups confectioner's sugar
   ½ cup cocoa
2. Then add:
   ¼ cup boiling water
   1 teaspoon vanilla
3. Spread mix on brownies.
4. Place walnut halves on each brownie to give the appearance of "bat wings."

VAMPIRE BLOOD PUNCH

1. Combine in a punch bowl
   2 cans fruit punch (12 oz. frozen or 46 oz. liquid)
   2-liter bottle ginger ale (sugarless)
2. Stir carefully and add ice.

TRICK-OR-TREAT PUNCH

1. Place a scoop of orange sherbet in each glass.
2. Slowly pour chilled, sugarless lemon-lime soda into glasses.
3. Add a straw and serve.
4. For a punch bowl, add one carton of sherbet to 3 quarts of soda.

JUMBO JACK-O'-LANTERN COOKIES

1. Turn on oven to 350°.
2. Add to a large mixing bowl and beat until light and fluffy:
   1½ cups margarine
   1 cup sugar
   1½ cups brown sugar
   1 egg
   1 teaspoon vanilla
3. Mix together in a separate bowl these dry ingredients:
   2 cups oatmeal
   4 cups flour
   2 teaspoons cinnamon
   2 teaspoons baking soda
4. Stir into first mixture 1 can (16 oz.) pumpkin.
5. Add bowl of dry ingredients.
6. Use ¼ cup measuring cup to measure each jumbo cookie. Pat cookies down with a spatula.
7. Bake 15 minutes.
8. Frost and decorate when cooled.
9. This recipe makes about 34 large, filling cookies.

Arthur's Tooth

AUTHOR: Marc Brown

ILLUSTRATOR: Marc Brown

PUBLISHING INFORMATION:
Atlantic Monthly, PB, 1985, ISBN 0-87113-006-8
Little, Brown, 1986, PB, ISBN 0-316-11245-3

SUGGESTED AGES: 5–7

TOPIC: Losing teeth

THEME: Children are concerned about losing their first teeth, especially when others have already lost several.

Setting the Stage

How many of you have lost some teeth? How many of you have *not* lost any teeth? Do you wish you could quickly lose one of your teeth or do you care that much?

Bridge

In the story *Arthur's Tooth* by Marc Brown, we find that Arthur had a tooth problem. What do you think that problem was? Let's see if some of your guesses happen in the story.

Discussion Questions

Significant Detail:
How did Arthur's friends offer to help him lose his baby teeth? (Buster brought carrots; the Brain invented a special machine; and Binky Barnes offered to knock out the tooth.)

Personal Relevance:
Would you enjoy having a friend like Francine? Tell why you feel that way.

Personal Prophecy:
What if Francine had not lost any baby teeth and Arthur had lost several? Tell how you think she might have acted.

Personal Relevance:
Arthur had a very scary picture in his mind about going to the dentist. Tell what it's really like to go to the dentist.

Logical Deduction:
What did Arthur mean when he told Francine that hitting him was the nicest thing she had ever done? (It caused him finally to lose a tooth.)

Activities

Science Experiment:
Prepare an experiment to demonstrate the effects of nutrition on teeth. Place teeth (dentists will sometimes give them to schools) in various liquids, including cola, milk, fruit juice, candy dissolved in water, coffee, and the like. Leave the teeth in the liquids for two weeks. Describe what happened to each tooth. Then mount the teeth with rubber cement on a large poster board and label them according to the liquid used.

Writing:
Brainstorm words related to dental health. Then create word pictures in the shape of a tooth.

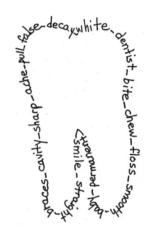

Children will enjoy filling out the simple crossword puzzle in Activity 6. Here are the answers:

ACROSS	DOWN
1. Loose	2. Sozio
3. D. W.	4. Baby
4. Buster	5. Francine

Young children will be interested in making their own dental charts by following the directions in Activity 7. Be prepared for lots of wet fingers!

Directions:

Use the Across and Down clues to fill in the boxes in the puzzle. The words to be used are listed below.

ACROSS

1. Arthur had a _____ tooth.

3. The name of Arthur's sister

4. Who brought carrots for Arthur's lunch?

DOWN

2. The name of Arthur's dentist

4. Arthur had _____ teeth.

5. Who accidently knocked out Arthur's tooth?

Word List

SOZIO

D.W.

FRANCINE

LOOSE

BUSTER

BABY

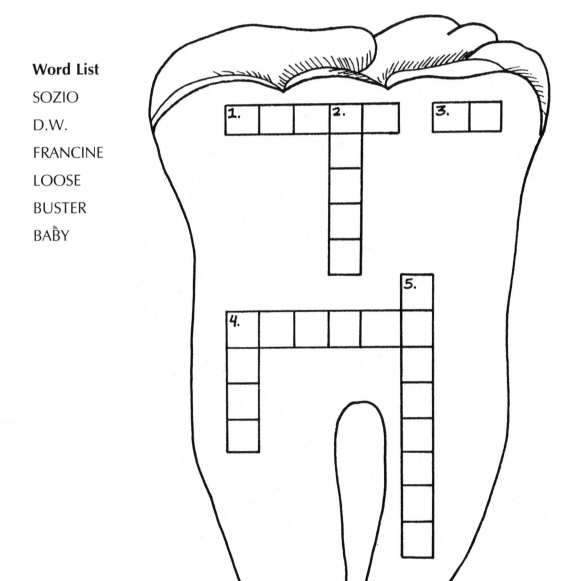

Arthur's Tooth

1. Color the spaces of missing teeth *black*.

2. Color the baby teeth *pink*.

3. Color the permanent teeth *red*.

Upper Teeth

Lower Teeth

From *After the Story's Over: Your Enrichment Guide to 88 Read-Aloud Children's Classics*, published by Scott, Foresman and Company. Copyright © 1991 Linda K. Garrity.

Arthur's Valentine

AUTHOR: Marc Brown

ILLUSTRATOR: Marc Brown

PUBLISHING INFORMATION:
Little, Brown, 1980, HB, ISBN 0-316-11062-0
Avon Camelot, 1982, PB, ISBN 0-380-57075-0
   (Snuggle & Read)
Little, Brown, 1988, PB, ISBN 0-316-11187-2

SUGGESTED AGES: 5–7

TOPICS: Candy
   Valentine's Day

THEME: Romantic teasing is very irritating to young children.

Setting the Stage

What do you like best about Valentine's Day? What do you dislike about Valentine's Day? (Since the pun in this story involves Hershey's kisses, it would be very appropriate to distribute a chocolate kiss to each child before the story.)

Bridge

Our friend Arthur has a big problem with Valentine's Day. Can you guess what it might be? Let's listen to Marc Brown's story to see if you are right and find out how Arthur finally solved his Valentine's Day problem.

Discussion Questions

Personal Relevance:
Do you decorate valentine boxes or bags and exchange valentines in your classroom? Do you have any rules about valentines? Why do you think that rule/s is/are necessary? (To avoid hurt feelings.)

Logical Deduction:
What do you think the teacher could have done so that Arthur wouldn't have had this problem in the first place? (Set up a one valentine per child rule.)

Personal Judgment:
Do you think Arthur was more upset because he knew Sue Ellen didn't like him and he had liked her, or because the other kids teased him and laughed about being in love? Why do you think that way?

Personal Relevance:
Teasing was a big problem for Arthur. It can be a big problem for lots of children. What do you do when other children tease you about something?

Significant Detail:
What kind of kisses did Arthur have for Francine? (candy Hershey's kisses) What did Francine think she was getting? (a real kiss)

Logical Deduction:
Why was that trick a better way of getting even with Francine than yelling or hitting her? (It didn't hurt her and it was funny, yet made her feel foolish just as she had made Arthur feel foolish and embarrassed.)

Activities

Poetry:
"Won't You," by Shel Silverstein, from *Where the Sidewalk Ends*, page 112, is a valentine poem that Arthur could have sent Sue Ellen.

Can you buy kisses? Arthur certainly did. Here's an amusing poem about kisses, from *The Random House Book of Poetry for Children*, page 103. Decide what kind of kisses the poet is talking about.

"Huckleberry, Gooseberry, Raspberry Pie," by Clyde Watson

Here are some other short, funny poems for Valentine's Day, from the same book:

"I Love You," Anonymous
"Question," Anonymous
"I Saw a Little Girl I Hate," Arnold Spilka

From *After the Story's Over: Your Enrichment Guide to 88 Read-Aloud Children's Classics*, published by Scott, Foresman and Company. Copyright © 1991 Linda K. Garrity.

Crafts:

The Arthur valentine is a clever project for children. See Activity 8. The silhouettes involve more effort but make nice keepsakes for parents (see Figure 3). First you need to trace each child's profile on a sheet of 12″ × 18″ black construction paper. Use a bright lamp or overhead projector. The children can then finish the Valentine memento for parents.

Figure 3 _____

Directions:

Cut out your silhouette and glue it in the center of a 12″ × 18″ sheet of white construction paper. Decorate the border with pink and red hearts.

From *After the Story's Over: Your Enrichment Guide to 88 Read-Aloud Children's Classics,* published by Scott, Foresman and Company. Copyright © 1991 Linda K. Garrity.

Directions:

Make an Arthur Valentine. Color the Valentine and cut out the oval.
Cut out both pieces and fasten together with a brass fastener at the ✳ .

A Baby Sister for Frances

AUTHOR: Russell Hoban

ILLUSTRATOR: Russell Hoban

PUBLISHING INFORMATION:
Harper & Row, 1964, HB, ISBN 0-06-022335-9
Harper & Row, 1964, LB, ISBN 0-06-022336-7
Harper Trophy, 1976, PB, ISBN 0-06-443006-5

SUGGESTED AGES: 5–6

TOPIC: Siblings

THEME: Young children often feel neglected when a new baby seems to dominate the household.

Setting the Stage

Why does it take so much time to care for new babies? What has to be done for them?

Bridge

Look at our cover. In this story Frances gets a new baby sister. How do you think Frances will handle that? Let's listen to see if you are right.

Discussion Questions

Significant Detail:
Why was Frances annoyed with her mother? (Her mother was so busy with the new baby that she didn't buy raisins for Frances's cereal or launder her blue dress.)

Main Idea:
Why did these things bother Frances so much? (She felt her mother was neglecting her for the new baby.)

Significant Detail:
How did Frances solve her problem? (She packed a knapsack and ran away to a spot under the dining room table.)

Logical Deduction:
Do you think Mother and Father were really lonely for Frances after she ran away? (No.) Why do you think so? (By the looks on their faces and the fact that she was just in the next room.)

Personal Prophecy:
If you had been Frances's mother or father, would you have been as patient with Frances or would you have scolded her and expected her to adjust better to the baby? Why do you feel that way?

Logical Deduction:
Do you think Mother and Father would have been so patient if Frances had run away to some place away from their home?

Significant Detail:
What extra treat did Mother promise to make if Frances would come home? (Chocolate cake.)

Main Idea:
Why do you think Frances decided that it wouldn't be so bad being a big sister? (She would have advantages, such as more allowance and chocolate cake.)

Activities

Poetry:
"The Runaway," by Bobbi Katz, from *The Random House Book of Poetry for Children*, page 138, is a poem that describes a child very much like Frances.

Don't you think Frances would agree with the poem "Some Things Don't Make Any Sense at All," by Judith Viorst, from the *Random House Book of Poetry for Children*, page 135?

"My Baby Brother," by Jack Prelutsky, from *The New Kid on the Block*, page 61, is a good description of a brand-new baby. Maybe the poet had a new baby at home.

Craft:
A simple knapsack is fun for young children to make. See Activity 9.

Drama:

This story is fun to act out. A few simple props, such as a doll for the baby, a pipe for Father, and some tables and chairs plus the knapsack from the craft project should suffice.

Writing:

Have children think of an appealing place to go for a trip and all the things they would like to take along. Explain the concept of a checklist and boxes to check off. See Activity 9.

Directions:

Color and cut out the knapsack. Fold on dotted lines. Cut slits to tuck tab into. Glue inside the two open edges to make a pocket with a flap. Punch holes where shown, and tie a piece of yarn or string for a strap. Draw, color, and cut out your favorite things to go inside the knapsack. Where are you going? What do you need? Fill out your checklist as you plan your trip.

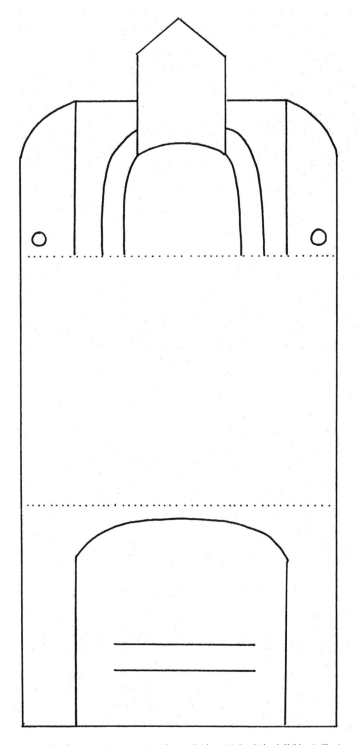

I'm going on a trip
to _____
This is my checklist
of things I need.

☐ _____

☐ _____

☐ _____

☐ _____

☐ _____

☐ _____

☐ _____

☐ _____

☐ _____

☐ _____

☐ _____

☐ _____

☐ _____

☐ _____

Bah! Humbug?

AUTHOR: Lorna Balian

ILLUSTRATOR: Lorna Balian

PUBLISHING INFORMATION:
Abingdon, 1982, HB, ISBN 0-687-02345-9
Abingdon, 1982, LB, ISBN 0-687-37107-4

SUGGESTED AGES: 5–8

TOPICS: Christmas
Siblings

THEME: Magic only comes to those who believe in it.

Setting the Stage

Do any of you have older brothers? How do they usually convince you to go along with their plans and schemes?

Bridge

On the cover of our story is a little girl named Margie. Her older brother, Arthur, has some interesting ways to get her to go along with his schemes. I wonder what he does. What do you think the title *Bah! Humbug?* means? Let's listen to Lorna Balian's Christmas story to find the answer to these questions.

Discussion Questions

Significant Detail:
What does Arthur threaten Margie with to get her to do what he wants? (He'll put worms in her bed, ice cubes in her pajamas, flush Herold down the toilet, stick bubble gum in her hair, and mush peanut butter and jelly all over Herold's new fur coat.)

Personal Prophecy:
What would you have done about Arthur's threats if you had been Margie?

Personal Prophecy:
What do you think the parents would have done if they had heard Arthur's threats?

Personal Judgment:
Do you think parents should try to control how brothers and sisters get along or just let children work things out themselves? Explain why you think that way.

Main Idea:
Why do you think only Margie got to see Santa Claus? (Because she believed in him.)

Significant Detail:
How was Herold's fur problem solved? You must look very closely at the wordless pages to see this. (Herold saw a replacement bear that was probably intended for Margie and another doll with a fur coat in Santa's sack. So Herold took the doll's fur coat and put it on himself.)

Activities

Poetry:
Margie and her brother got ready for Santa and then had to wait. This poem, "From: A Christmas Package," by David McCord, which is from *The Random House Book of Poetry for Children*, page 49, tells about another little boy who has made his preparations and is waiting.

Craft:
Make a Christmas stocking. You can use red and green felt for this project. See Activity 10.

Directions:

Use this pattern to design and color your own Christmas stocking. Cut out two pieces from construction paper or felt. Sew them together with yarn. Add trim such as glitter, tinsel, or cut-out letters of your name.

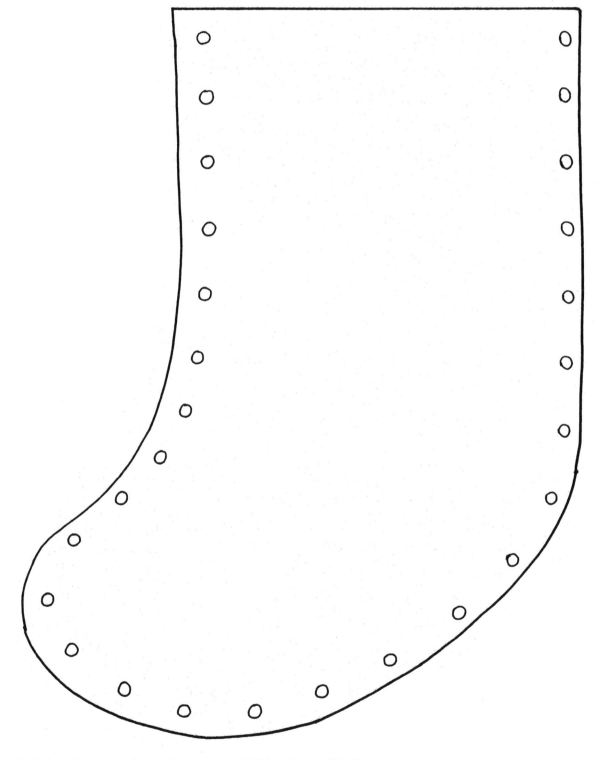

Bedtime for Frances

AUTHOR: Russell Hoban

ILLUSTRATOR: Garth Williams

PUBLISHING INFORMATION:
Harper & Row, 1960, HB, ISBN 0-06-022350-2
Harper & Row, 1960, LB, ISBN 0-06-022351-0
Harper Trophy, 1975, PB, ISBN 0-06-443005-7

SUGGESTED AGES: 5–6

TOPICS: Bedtime
Fear of dark
Monsters

THEME: Children will try to put off bedtime as long as they can.

Setting the Stage

Do you hate to go to bed at night? What do you do to put it off?

Bridge

Frances is not very interested in going to bed either. She does a number of things to avoid going to sleep. Let's listen to see what she does in *Bedtime for Frances*, by Russell Hoban.

Discussion Questions

Significant Details:
What different creatures did Frances think were in her room? (A tiger and a giant.)
  What did Frances see her parents eating after she had gone to bed? (Cake and tea.)

Personal Relevance:
Do your parents sometimes have special snacks after you've gone to bed?

Personal Judgment:
Do you think it is all right for parents to have special treats or do you think they should share everything with their children?

Main Idea:
Why did Frances finally fall asleep? (She was tired from all the stalling and also she didn't want to get spanked.)

Personal Relevance:
Would your parents have put up with as much delay from you over going to bed as Frances's parents did? How would they have treated Frances?

Activities

Creative Thinking:
The alphabet song could be made into an oral activity for the entire class or it could be used as the basis for a class book, with each child contributing one line on an illustrated page.

Writing:
Children could draw or write about scary things that they see in their rooms at night.

Drama:
A few props such as blankets and pillows and a pipe for father help children to act out this story.

Craft:
Children can use their creativity for the drawings in Activity 11. Discuss the project beforehand so they will put thought and detail into their drawings.

Directions:

Frances is scared by the crack in her ceiling. Add to these cracks to make scary monsters.

From *After the Story's Over: Your Enrichment Guide to 88 Read-Aloud Children's Classics*, published by Scott, Foresman and Company. Copyright © 1991 Linda K. Garrity.

The Berenstain Bears Go to School

AUTHOR: Stan and Jan Berenstain

ILLUSTRATOR: Stan and Jan Berenstain

PUBLISHING INFORMATION:
Random House, 1978, LB, ISBN 0-394-93736-8
Random House, 1978, PB, ISBN 0-394-83736-3

SUGGESTED AGES: 5–6

TOPICS: School
Siblings

THEME: Many children feel anxious about going to school for the first time.

Setting the Stage

All of you had ideas about what school would be like before you started. What ideas were "way off"? What ideas were pretty close? We all wonder and sometimes worry about new experiences before they happen. (The adult should share some preconceived notions about being a parent or teacher.)

Bridge

Boys and girls always enjoy hearing the adventures of the Berenstain Bears. Let's find out what happens when *The Berenstain Bears Go to School*.

Discussion Questions

Significant Detail:
In the beginning of the story, which bear was the most worried about school? (Sister.)

Main Idea:
Why was Sister Bear worried? (She disliked the idea of leaving her family, friends, and toys; she was also nervous about the unknown.)

Logical Deduction:
Why were the smaller bears so quiet on the bus? (They were afraid.)

Personal Prophecy:
If you had been Sister Bear and you noticed a small bear next to you on the bus who was afraid, what would you have done?

Significant Details:
Who had a hard time getting excited about school near the end of the story? (Brother Bear.)

What did Sister Bear do about it? (She told him that school was fun and they needed to get going.)

Personal Relevance:
When did you first start to feel comfortable about going to school?

Activities

Every activity in school has a purpose. Some things that children do are more fun than others, though everything has an important reason. List school activities on the blackboard in two categories: things that children enjoy about school and things that they don't enjoy. Note that the same activity will frequently go in both categories. Then have children explain the purpose of each activity. This is a very worthwhile exercise—illuminating for both child and adult.

Craft:
Children enjoy drawing their friends in the school bus in Activity 12.

Activity 12

Name _____

Directions:

Draw pictures of yourself, your friends, and Brother and Sister Bear riding together in the bus to school. Don't forget the driver!

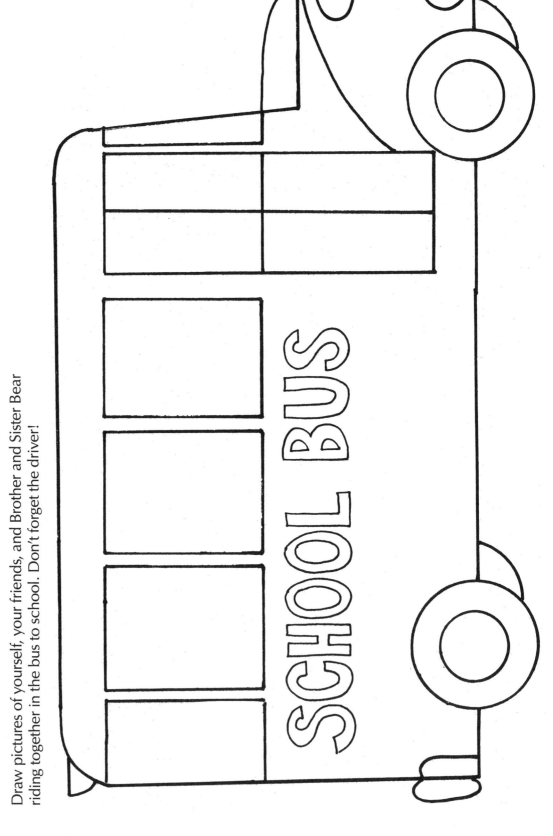

SCHOOL BUS

Best Friends

AUTHOR: Steven Kellogg

ILLUSTRATOR: Steven Kellogg

PUBLISHING INFORMATION:
Dial Books, 1986, HB ISBN 0-8037-0099-7
Dial Books, 1986, LB, ISBN 0-8037-0101-2

SUGGESTED AGES: 6–9

TOPIC: Friends

THEME: Disagreements are a natural part of children's friendships.

Setting the Stage

Even the best of friends sometimes have disagreements or fights. What are some of the things children fight about?

Bridge

Judging from the cover of Steven Kellogg's book *Best Friends*, I'd say this was a wild story! Let's see what all this has to do with the ups and downs of the friendship between two girls.

Discussion Questions

Significant Detail:
What imaginary play idea did the girls enjoy? (They pretended that they had a magic horse named Golden Silverwind that lived between their homes.)

Personal Relevance:
When I was a child, may favorite imaginary game was . . . What is yours?

Logical Deductions:
Why did Kathy get so mad at Louise? (She was jealous of all the fun and new friends that Louise was enjoying.)
  Do you think Kathy's mom understood the problem? (Yes.)

Significant Detail:
What did Kathy's mom suggest that she do? (She suggested Kathy try not to be jealous and see if there might be a new neighbor or playmate.)

Personal Relevance:
When you have a problem with friends, what kind of help or advice does your mom or dad offer?

Kathy did not think that an older man would be a good friend at all, but she discovered that she had misjudged him. Have you ever had a friend who was much older or different from you in some other way?

Logical Deduction:
Why do you think Kathy did not tell Louise that she had been mad at her? (She was ashamed to admit that she had been jealous.)

Personal Prophecy:
When the girls discovered that there would be only one puppy, it was upsetting. What would you have done if you had been Louise? What would you have done if you had been Kathy?

Activities

Craft:
Younger children will enjoy the coloring page on friends. See Activity 13.

Writing:
All ages of children can write about the difficulties of making and keeping friends.

Writing:
Older children could design employment applications for the characters in the story, as well as for themselves.

Drama:
Children enjoy impromptu skits showing how to make new friends and how to handle disagreements between friends.

From *After the Story's Over: Your Enrichment Guide to 88 Read-Aloud Children's Classics,* published by Scott, Foresman and Company. Copyright © 1991 Linda K. Garrity.

Directions:

Fill in the information on your friends. Then color the page.

My best friend is:

_____

I have many friends.
Some of my friends are:

_____   _____

_____

The Biggest House in the World

AUTHOR: Leo Lionni

ILLUSTRATOR: Leo Lionni

PUBLISHING INFORMATION:
Pantheon Books, 1968, HB, ISBN 0-394-90944-5
Knopf, 1987, PB, ISBN 0-317-53625-7
Knopf Dragonfly, 1987, PB, ISBN 0-394-82740-6

SUGGESTED AGES: 5–7, 8–9
(This story can be used with a wider range of ages if the corresponding questions presented in this book unit are used.)

TOPICS: Fables
Houses

THEME: Be content with what you have.

Following is a questioning model for younger children:

Setting the Stage

What are some nice things that are little?

Bridge

Today's story is called a fable. That means a short story that will teach you something. Let's listen to this story and see what you learn.

Discussion Questions

Main Idea:
What did the little snail learn? (Be content with what you have, or, some things are better small.)

Personal Relevance:
Most parents are like the snail's father. They try to tell their children how to behave so they will grow up to be nice people. What do your parents tell you?

Following is a questioning model for eight- and nine-year-olds:

Setting the Stage

Have you ever heard the expression, "Great things come in small packages"? What are some special things that are small?

Bridge

Today's story is a fable. What makes a fable different from other types of stories? A fable is a short story, usually with animals as the characters, that teaches us a lesson. Leo Lionni is a modern-day writer (unlike Aesop, who lived long ago) who primarily writes fables for children. Let's listen for the moral or lesson as we look at the outstanding illustrations in *The Biggest House in the World*.

Discussion Questions

Main Idea:
What is the moral of the story? (Be content with what you have, or, some things are better small.)

Personal Judgment:
Other famous expressions or morals are: "Pride goeth before a fall," and "The higher they climb, the harder they fall." What do these expressions mean? Which one do you think fits the story best? Why do you think that way?

Personal Relevance:
Like the snail parents in the story, real parents often teach their children by using expressions. What expressions do your parents say? What do they mean?

Personal Judgment:
Often parents and teachers tell children to give life their very best and try to be all they can be. Do you think that attitude conflicts with the moral of Lionni's story? Which slogan do you personally believe in most: "Be content with what you have" or "Be all you can be"?

Activities

Poetry:
Maybe snails dream of all sorts of things. What unusual dream did the snail have in "The Snails' Dream," by Oliver Herford, from *The Random House Book of Poetry for Children*, page 183?

Writing:
Proverbs are old sayings or expressions used to give people guidance. They are found at the end of fables. Children can write a fable using a proverb if they have a clear understanding of the proverb beforehand. Following are some fairly explicit to choose from:

Waste not, want not.
Two heads are better than one.
Look before you leap.
One good turn deserves another.
Provide for the future.
Slow and steady wins the race.
Work before play.
No one believes a liar.
Try to please everyone, and you will please no one.

A Birthday for Frances

AUTHOR: Russell Hoban

ILLUSTRATOR: Russell Hoban

PUBLISHING INFORMATION:
Harper & Row, 1968, HB, ISBN 0-06-022338-3
Harper & Row, 1968, LB, ISBN 0-06-022339-1
Harper Trophy, 1976, PB, ISBN 0-06-443007-3

SUGGESTED AGES: 5–6

TOPICS: Birthdays
Siblings

THEME: It is difficult for young children to take a back seat to the birthday child.

Setting the Stage

How do you feel when other children in your family have a birthday and everything is very special for them?

Bridge

Gloria, who is Frances's little sister, has a birthday, complete with a party. I wonder why the story is called *A Birthday for Frances*? Let's listen and see if we can figure this title out.

Discussion Questions

Logical Deduction:
In the beginning Frances spelled words rather than saying them. Did she spell them correctly? (No.) How can you tell? (The letters didn't match the beginning sounds.) Why did she do that? (Maybe she thought she could show her mom that she could "talk over her head.")

Personal Relevance:
Do your parents spell words or speak in a different language so they can "talk over your head"? Can you sometimes figure out what they are saying anyway?

Personal Judgment:
Which do you think would be worse—for Frances to buy nothing for Gloria for her birthday or to buy treats for her and then eat them before the party?

Logical Deductions:
What made Frances change her mind about giving the candy to Gloria? (When Gloria wished that Frances would not be mad at her and apologized about the sandpail and shovel.)

If Frances got a nickel and two pennies for her allowance, and she spent two allowances on Gloria's gift, how much did she spend? (Fourteen cents.)

How do you think Frances's and Gloria's parents felt when Frances gladly gave Gloria the Chompo bar? (They felt proud of her generosity.)

Main Idea:
Do you think Mother and Father knew how Frances felt about the party and the attention that Gloria was receiving? (Yes.) What makes you think that way? (Expressions on the parent's faces and their comments; parents usually know what's going on.)

Personal Prophecy:
What would you have done about the birthday gift if you had been Frances? Would you have been as nice as Gloria?

Activities

Poetry:
Having a sister or brother forget your birthday would be pretty disgusting; at least that's what the boy thought in this poem, "I'm Disgusted with My Brother," by Jack Prelutsky, from *The New Kid on the Block*, page 128. However, he had a special reason to feel disgusted. Let's see why.

In "If We Didn't Have Birthdays," from *The Random House Book of Poetry for Children*, page 126, Dr. Seuss has written a very funny poem about birthdays. Even if you didn't know who wrote it, I'll bet you would guess Dr. Seuss!

One of the best parts of birthdays is the surprises. This poem, "Surprises," by Jean Conder Soule, from *The Random House Book of Poetry for Children*, page 126, is all about them!

From *After the Story's Over: Your Enrichment Guide to 88 Read-Aloud Children's Classics*, published by Scott, Foresman and Company. Copyright © 1991 Linda K. Garrity.

Drama:
Six children could dramatize the birthday party scene.

Cooking:
Here are some ideas for an "unbirthday" party at the end of the year for children with summer birthdays or for unusual party refreshments at home.

UNBIRTHDAY CAKE
1. Slice an angel food cake into thin slices.
2. Allow 2 or 3 slices per child.
3. Use the Unbirthday Icing recipe to create colorful icing.
4. Frost each piece with a different color and stack them for an individual cake.
5. The icing colors and the ice cubes can be color-coordinated for a festive look.

UNBIRTHDAY ICING
1. Add to a medium-sized mixing bowl and beat until fluffy:
   2 sticks softened margarine
   4 cups confectioner's sugar
   2 teaspoons vanilla
   2 tablespoons milk
2. Divide the mix into small bowls and add a few drops of food coloring to each bowl. Use the guide on the back of the food coloring box to get combinations of exciting new colors.
3. Icing may be made in advance and refrigerated. Stir and start decorating!

UNBIRTHDAY PUNCH
1. Make different colored drink mixes (for example, red, purple, and green) according to the directions, but reduce the water by half.
2. Carefully pour the mixes into ice cube trays and freeze overnight.
3. Serve the colored ice cubes in clear glasses with a clear soda.
4. Using the same colors in one glass tastes best, but a combination is definitely exciting.
(5. If you use nonsugar drink mixes and soda, this can be a sugarless treat.)

Bread and Jam for Frances

AUTHOR: Russell Hoban

ILLUSTRATOR: Russell Hoban

PUBLISHING INFORMATION:
Harper & Row, 1964, HB, ISBN 0-06-022359-6
Harper & Row, 1964, LB, ISBN 0-06-022360-X
Harper Trophy, 1986, PB, ISBN 0-06-443096-0

SUGGESTED AGES: 5–7

TOPICS: Eating habits
Food

THEMES: There can be too much of a good thing. It is not logical to judge a food without tasting it first.

Setting the Stage

Do you like or dislike eggs? (The adult should describe a variety of egg dishes.) What kinds do you especially like or dislike?

Bridge

Frances has a difficult time with eggs. She has a reason for disliking each different type of egg dish. Look at the cover. What do you think Frances does like to eat? I wonder what her parents think about this. Let's find out in *Bread and Jam for Frances*, by Russell Hoban.

Discussion Questions

Significant Detail:
Why didn't Frances like soft-boiled eggs? (They slid around.)

Logical Deduction:
Was it the taste of the eggs that she disliked or their texture (the way they felt)? (It was their texture.)

Personal Judgment:
Which do you dislike more in foods—strange textures (such as lumpy, gooey, or slippery) or strange tastes? Name some foods you dislike and then decide if the problem lies with the taste or the texture.

Personal Prophecy:
If you had been Frances's mother, how would you have handled Frances's eating problem?

Personal Relevance:
What do your parents do or say when you dislike some food that is served?

Significant Detail:
What did Frances say when Mother served her bread and jam instead of letting her try the spaghetti and meatballs? ("How do you know what I'll like if you won't even try me?")

Who had said something like that earlier? (Father.) What did he say? ("How do you know what you'll like if you won't even try anything?")

Main Idea:
Who do you think was right: Frances, Father, or both of them? (Both of them were right.) Why? (They were saying the same thing.)

Activities

Poetry:
Listen to this poem about eggs. Would Jack Prelutsky, who wrote "Eggs," from *The New Kid on the Block*, page 104, agree or disagree with Frances about eating eggs?

"Jellyfish Stew," also by Jack Prelutsky, from *The New Kid on the Block*, page 8, would be a food with both a strange texture and a strange taste. Listen to decide if Frances (or you) would like this dish.

Does this poem by Prelutsky—"I'd Never Eat a Beet," from *The New Kid on the Block*, page 124—sound like one that Frances would enjoy?

Show children the "Ghost-buster" sign in the upper corner of page 124. In a drawing activity have them make similar signs for the foods they dislike .

In "Egg Thoughts," from *The Random House Book of Poetry for Children*, page 147, Russell Hoban has written a poem that expresses Frances's thoughts about eggs.

From *After the Story's Over: Your Enrichment Guide to 88 Read-Aloud Children's Classics*, published by Scott, Foresman and Company. Copyright © 1991 Linda K. Garrity.

Another funny poem about children eating eggs is called "Little Bits of Soft-Boiled Egg," by Fay Maschler, from *The Random House Book of Poetry for Children*, page 149.

Drama:

Individual children can role-play how they behave, both at home and away from home, when they are served food they dislike.

Cooking:

Following are some ideas for different ways to fix Frances's favorite food:

ANIMAL SNACKERS

1. Use a cookie cutter to cut a shape out of a slice of bread.
2. Spread the bread with cream cheese that has been colored or flavored by stirring in a few drops of food coloring.

3. Some garnishes that you can serve to make the animals' faces are:

   Triangle cheese or melon slices for ears and noses

   Raisins, pickle slices, boiled egg slices, olive slices, and radish slices for eyes

   Shredded carrots for fur or manes.

   Pretzels for whiskers.

   Apple and celery slices for mouths.

   Use your imagination!

For dessert Frances might enjoy the following:

BREAD AND JAM ROLL-UPS

1. Cut the crusts off a slice of brown or white bread.
2. Gently flatten the slice with a rolling pin.
3. Spread it with peanut butter and your favorite jam. Add banana slices if you like.
4. Roll up tightly and fasten with two toothpicks.

A Chair for My Mother

AUTHOR: Vera B. Williams

ILLUSTRATOR: Vera B. Williams

PUBLISHING INFORMATION:
Greenwillow, 1982, HB, ISBN 0-688-00914-X
Greenwillow, 1982, LB, ISBN 0-688-00915-8
Greenwillow, 1984, PB, ISBN 0-688-04074-8

SUGGESTED AGES: 6–9

TOPICS: Chairs
Families

THEMES: Catastrophes bring out charity in people. Waiting and saving for an item gives it added meaning.

Setting the Stage

It's fun to shop for something new. What do you like to buy with your own money? What do you like to shop for with your parents? Saving money for a big item is difficult to do. Are you saving for something right now? What is it? How much will you need?

Bridge

The family in today's story saved for a long time for a big item. Look at the title. What do you think the item will be? Yes, *A Chair for My Mother.* I wonder why the mother needed a chair. Let's listen to Vera Williams's story to find out more about this chair.

Discussion Questions

Main Idea:
Do you think if Mama had gone right down to the store after the fire and bought a new chair, it would have had as much meaning? (No, saving and waiting made it more special.)

Logical Deduction:
Why did Mama want a comfortable chair so much? (She was tired after working as a waitress all day, and they had lost their other chairs in the fire.)

Why would a waitress be quite tired and have sore feet at night? (It's hard work, walking and standing all the time.)

Why do you think the family didn't just take the jar of coins to the furniture store? (It was too heavy, embarrassing to have the store people know they had to save coins, too time-consuming to count.)

Personal Relevance:
Have you ever shopped in a furniture store? It's important that furniture you buy be comfortable, isn't it? However, what do you have to be careful of, while you are trying out furniture?

Logical Deduction:
Why wouldn't Mama let the little girl ride in the chair in the back of the truck while Uncle Sandy was driving the truck home? (It would be too dangerous; she could have fallen out onto the street.)

Significant Deduction:
After the fire, what did the neighbors and relatives do? (Brought the family food and furnishings for their new apartment.)

Main Idea:
Why do you think those people were so kind and generous? (Someone else's catastrophe brings out the best in people; maybe they felt sorry for the family.)

Personal Prophecy:
If you lost all your possessions (not people or pets), in a fire, what would you want to replace most?

Activities

Writing:
A Mother's Day activity could involve writing a cinquain about the mother in the story or a child's own mother or grandmother. The pattern for a cinquain is:

From *After the Story's Over: Your Enrichment Guide to 88 Read-Aloud Children's Classics,* published by Scott, Foresman and Company. Copyright © 1991 Linda K. Garrity.

Noun (the title—2 syllables)
Two adjectives (describe the title—4 syllables)
Three ''ing'' verbs (express actions—6 syllables)
A thought (expresses a feeling—8 syllables
A synonym for the noun in line 1 (2 syllables)

Here is an example of a cinquain:

> Mom's hands
> Weathered, skillful
> Cleaning, cooking, sewing
> Time for rest in eternity
> Helpers

A fitting poetry book filled with well-written and beautifully illustrated poems about all kinds of mothers is *Poems for Mothers*, selected by Myra Cohn Livingston, Holiday House, New York, 1988.

A simple, yet interesting activity would be to have children interview an adult about an item that he or she really wanted and saved for at some point in his or her life. They could then share their interviews with the class.

Children can compose an imaginary shopping list for people in their family. For younger children, money would not figure into their plans. For older children, a variety of financial parameters could be established, such as an overall price limit or an individual family member price limit. Mail-order catalogues with indexes can help children determine prices. This activity not only is fun for children but also teaches them the use of an index, mathematics, and decision-making.

Cloudy with a Chance of Meatballs

AUTHOR: Judi Barrett

ILLUSTRATOR: Ron Barrett

PUBLISHING INFORMATION:
Atheneum, 1978, HB, ISBN 0-689-30647-4
Aladdin, 1982, PB, ISBN 0-689-70749-5

SUGGESTED AGES: 5–8

TOPICS: Food
Grandfathers

THEME: There can be too much of a good thing.

Setting the Stage

What is your favorite drink? What if the school's drinking fountains were full of your favorite drink, instead of water? Do you think that might cause a problem?

Bridge

Something similar to that situation happened in this hilarious story by Judi and Ron Barrett. Let's look at what happens in *Cloudy with a Chance of Meatballs*.

Discussion Questions

Significant Details:
Is this a true story or is it made-up? (It is made-up.) How can you tell? (It's totally illogical.)

What gave Grandpa the idea for the story? (The pancake incident at breakfast.) The story sounds a little like what part of the nightly news? (The weather forecast.) From what other places do you think Grandpa got story ideas? (Television.)

Logical Deduction:
Some foods would work better than others if they came from the sky. What would be some foods that would work pretty well? (Solid, lightweight, room temperature foods.) What are some foods that would work poorly? (Liquids, heavy foods.) What foods would be dangerous? (Heavy foods, such as some fruits and vegetables; hot liquids; frozen foods; syrupy foods.)

Main Idea:
What caused the marvelous food situation at Chewandswallow to go bad? (Too much food.)

Personal Prophecy:
If you had been the mayor of Chewandswallow, what would you have done to control the situation so the people could have stayed?

Activities

Poetry:
What is confetti? To match our silly spaghetti story, we have "Spaghetti," a silly spaghetti poem by Shel Silverstein, from *Where the Sidewalk Ends*, page 100. Another poem by Silverstein that brings to mind our story is "Sky Seasoning," from *Where the Sidewalk Ends*, page 31.

The town of Chewandswallow was pretty wacky! The following poem, "The Folk Who Live in Backward Town," by Mary Ann Hoberman, from *The Random House Book of Poetry for Children*, page 181, describes a different town that is just as zany.

Writing:
Older children could study weather forecasts in the newspaper and on the television news and try to write their own forecasts using different foods.

Cooking:
The recipe will make enough for a small serving for each child in the class.

CLOUDY WITH A CHANCE OF FRUITBALLS
1. Stir together until well blended:
   1 cup orange juice
   2 cups unflavored yogurt
   ½ cup sugar
   1 teaspoon grated orange peel
2. Add 3 cups of diced fresh fruit, including some berries
3. Serve in small cups or bowls.
4. The mixture can also be chilled and served later.

Craft:

Have a small committee study the illustrations for ideas and then design a large mural of the town of Chewandswallow. They could create streets, parks, and lots for the buildings, assigning the construction of the buildings to the rest of the class through a system such as a secret drawing. After the children made their paper buildings, such as homes, shops, and public buildings, the committee would paste the structures into position on the mural. The committee would need to be specific about the size of the proposed buildings in order to maintain the scale of the project. Committee members would also need to consider factors, such as number of children in the class and the buildings and functions that are necessary for a community to exist.

The Cobweb Christmas

AUTHOR: Shirley Climo

ILLUSTRATOR: Joe Lasker

PUBLISHING INFORMATION:
Crowell, 1982, HB, ISBN 0-690-04215-9
Harper & Row, 1982, LB, ISBN 0-690-04216-7
Harper Trophy, 1986, PB, ISBN 0-06-443110-X

SUGGESTED AGES: 6–8

TOPIC: Christmas

THEMES: It is natural to be curious about the unknown.
The origin of Christmas tree tinsel is the basis of this magical story.

Setting the Stage

At Christmas or Chanukah time my family . . . (Explain a holiday custom from your childhood.) Since we did that every year, it is called a custom. What holiday custom does your family observe?

Bridge

Where do you suppose the old lady on our cover is going? What do you think she is going to do with that ax? Let's find out if your ideas are right and, at the same time, let's see what Christmas customs she observes.

Discussion Questions

Significant Details:
What Christmas custom did Tante observe? (She made gingerbread boys and girls, baked almond and cinnamon cookies, hung apples on the tree, and prepared various treats for all the animals but the spiders.)

Who was Christkindel? (The spirit who went from house to house on Christmas Eve and slipped presents into the toes of children's shoes.)

Logical Deduction:
What similar person do many American children wait for on Christmas Eve? (Santa Claus)

This story happened in Germany. What Christmas customs there are like ones in this country? What Christmas customs are different? (Baked cookies and trees are similar; Christkindel and stories of miracles are different.)

Main Idea:
Why did the spiders want to join in? (They were curious about the celebration of Christmas.)

Significant Detail:
Why had the spiders always been left out? (They had always been swept away during the house cleaning.)

Personal Prophecy:
If you had been Christkindel, what would you have done when the spiders asked to come in?

Personal Relevance:
Have you ever been curious about something and later found out about it? Tell about that experience. (The adult should relate an experience here to start off the discussion.)

Main Ideas:
What was the Christmas miracle? (Because Christkindel was worried that Tante would feel badly about all the webs on her tree, he changed them to silver and gold.)

How did that Christmas miracle become a custom for Tante? (She always wove tinsel among the branches of her Christmas tree, and she always left a few webs around so the spiders could enjoy Christmas also.)

Personal Judgment:
Do you think this story is true or made-up? Why do you think that?

Activities

Poetry:
Spiders aren't the only creatures who want to celebrate Christmas. Listen to this clever poem—"Merry Christmas," by Aileen Fisher, from *The Random House Book of Poetry* for Children, page 49—and see if you can tell what type of writing the animal creates.

Craft:

Young children could make pinecone bird feeders to feed birds or small animals in the winter.

Merely stuff the cones with sunflower seeds, peanut butter, cheese, raisins, and other foods birds like and place the cones or hang them with string in an area where birds can feed from them.

Research:

What other Christmas customs are used in Germany or other countries? Older children could use the media center to research Christmas customs around the world and later share them with the rest of the class.

Cooking:

COBWEB CHRISTMAS TREES

1. In a large pan add:
   3 tablespoons butter or margarine
   3 cups miniature marshmallows
2. Turn burner on low and stir until melted.
3. Set pan on counter and stir in:
   ½ teaspoon green food coloring
   ½ teaspoon vanilla
4. Add, stirring gently:
   4 cups Cheerios
5. After the mixture has cooled enough to handle, dump about ⅓ cup of it onto waxed paper.
6. Coat fingers with a little soft margarine and shape the mixture into a tree.
7. Add a few red hots for ornaments!
8. Makes 24–30 trees.

Corduroy

AUTHOR: Don Freeman

ILLUSTRATOR: Don Freeman

PUBLISHING INFORMATION:
Viking, 1968, HB, ISBN 0-670-24133-4
Penguin Puffin, 1976, PB, ISBN 0-14-050173-8

SUGGESTED AGES: 5–6

TOPIC: Teddy bears

THEME: Children love their teddy bears.

Setting the Stage

Corduroy is the name of a little teddy bear in today's story. What is the name of your favorite teddy bear (or other stuffed animal)?

Bridge

Lisa, the little girl in *Corduroy*, wanted a teddy bear very much. What do you think she did to get her special bear? Let's listen to the story by Don Freeman to find out.

Discussion Questions

Significant Details:
Why didn't the mother want to buy the bear for Lisa? (She had spent too much money already and the bear didn't look new because he had lost a button to his overalls.)

How did Lisa solve the problem of buying the bear? (She came back the next day with her savings.)

Personal Prophecy:
How do you think some children might have reacted when the mother did not buy the bear?

Personal Relevance:
How would you have reacted?

Personal Prophecy:
Corduroy had some exciting adventures in the empty department store. Tell about another adventure that might have happened.

Significant Detail:
Corduroy told Lisa that he had always wanted two things. What were those two things? (A home and a new friend.)

Personal Judgment:
Which thing do *you* think Corduroy wanted most? Why do you feel that way?

Activities

Discuss the characteristics of corduroy fabric (warm, soft, cotton, has ridges). Provide a sample of the fabric for children to touch. Then allow children to handle other fabrics, such as silk or satin, nylon, wool, vinyl, and so on. Create a bag filled with various fabric swatches for children to handle with their eyes closed and identify.

Celebrate a Teddy Bear Day!
Let everyone bring in their favorite stuffed animal to introduce to the group. Name tags could be made, a parade held, and awards given for oldest, newest, largest, smallest, most beloved (worn), etc.

Craft:
The paper-doll outfits are neither feminine nor masculine, so both boys and girls can enjoy creating a wardrobe for Corduroy. Younger children who might have difficulty with the tabs could merely cut them off as they cut out the clothes and paste their favorite outfit on Corduroy. See Activity 14.

Drama:
Children could role-play shopping with a parent, showing good ways and poor ways to handle children's requests for purchases.

Directions:

Color Corduroy and cut him out. Color the clothes, adding other designs
and trims. Then cut out your bear's new wardrobe!

The Country Bunny and the Little Gold Shoes

AUTHOR: Du Bose Heyward

ILLUSTRATOR: Marjorie Flack

PUBLISHING INFORMATION:
Houghton Mifflin, 1939, LB,
ISBN 0-395-15990-3
Houghton Mifflin Sandpiper, 1974, PB,
ISBN 0-395-18557-2

SUGGESTED AGES: 5–8

TOPICS: Easter
Rabbits

THEMES: Mothers with young children are as capable as single men.
If properly trained, children can be very helpful with housework.

Setting the Stage

When your mother has something important coming up, like a meeting or company coming, what do you do to help her out?

Bridge

On the cover of our story we can see that this mother had quite a few children. Let's count them together to see exactly how many. Twenty-one bunnies! Their mother had something *very* important come up, and she needed her children to help her. Let's see what it was and how they were able to help their mother.

Discussion Questions

Significant Detail:
Why did the big white rabbits and the Jack Rabbits laugh at the country bunny? (They thought it was ridiculous for a brown country bunny with twenty-one children to want to be an Easter bunny.)

Main Idea:
How did the country bunny's large family help her become a good Easter bunny? (She had to have been wise and clever to have trained her children to do the housework and been kind to have raised such good-natured children, and she learned to be swift, playing tag with her children.)

Significant Detail:
What were all the household tasks that the children had learned to do? (Sweeping, bedmaking, cooking, doing dishes, tending the garden, doing laundry, mending, singing and dancing, painting pictures, and pulling out the chair for the mother.)

Personal Prophecy:
If you had been one of the bunnies, which household task do you think you would have liked learning to do? Why would you have preferred that one?

Personal Judgment:
Do you think all of the tasks took an equal amount of work? How do you think tasks should be divided up in a family to be fair to all? Remember things like age, ability, allowance, and amount of time needed.

Personal Relevance:
How is housework divided up in your family?

Personal Prophecy:
The Palace of Easter Eggs looks like a delightful place. If you could go on a tour and select Easter eggs for yourself, what type and flavor would you choose? (The adult should give an answer here also.)

Significant Details:
Why did Grandfather choose the country bunny for the best, but hardest trip? (Because she had such a loving heart for children.)

How was the country bunny finally able to get the special egg to the little boy? (Grandfather gave her a pair of magic gold shoes so she could fly up there and give the egg to the child before morning.)

Personal Prophecy:
Grandfather might have solved the problem with a different magic item other than the gold shoes. Tell about a magic item that could solve the problem.

From *After the Story's Over: Your Enrichment Guide to 88 Read-Aloud Children's Classics*, published by Scott, Foresman and Company. Copyright © 1991 Linda K. Garrity.

Personal Judgment:

If, in the future, a young mother bunny applies for an Easter bunny job, what do you think the big white rabbits and Jacks will say?

Activities

Poetry:

The Jack Rabbits were not the only creatures that thought a girl bunny could not handle an important job. These two poems —"Girls Can, Too!" by Lee Bennett Hopkins, and "No Girls Allowed," by Jack Prelutsky, from *The Random House Book of Poetry for Children,* page 111—tell about a similar attitude held by some boys.

Craft:

This project for older children makes elegant, though delicate eggs. See figure 4.

Writing:

The story appeals to younger children, yet its message is more appropriate for older youngsters. Older children can use their imagination to write an interview with the country bunny. They could draw a picture of the interviewee and then brainstorm questions, such as accomplishments, goals in life, hobbies, and favorite books, movies, and food.

The country bunny was deserving of several awards and medals. Children can decide what they should be and write them on the examples in Activity 15.

Figure 4 _____

SUGAR EGG WITH SCENE

1 large egg white
3 cups granulated sugar
large egg mold (2 halves)
tube for frosting

Mix ingredients with hands until moist. Press into both halves of mold. When outside edge has begun to harden, scoop out inside, leaving ½" walls. Be sure to scoop out one end completely for peephole.

side view

Draw a bunny on construction paper and color it. Glue the bunny on the bottom half of the egg. Add grass, flowers, and so on. When both halves are completely dry, glue them together. Decorate the outside with squiggles of frosting around the peephole and the glue line.

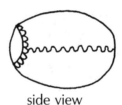

side view

Looking inside

Name _____

Activity 15

Country Bunny Awards and Medals

Directions:

Ribbons and awards for outstanding accomplishments are often given to people. In fact, you may have won a special ribbon or award yourself. Write in special awards or ribbons for the Country Bunny, based on her accomplishments in the story.

From *After the Story's Over: Your Enrichment Guide to 88 Read-Aloud Children's Classics*, published by Scott, Foresman and Company. Copyright © 1991 Linda K. Garrity.

Cranberry Thanksgiving

AUTHORS: Wende and Harry Devlin

ILLUSTRATORS: Wende and Harry Devlin

PUBLISHING INFORMATION:
Macmillan, 1971, 1980, HB, ISBN 0-02-729930-9

SUGGESTED AGES: 5–8

TOPICS: Food
Thanksgiving

THEMES: Appearances can be deceiving.
Forgiveness is an important, positive trait.

Setting the Stage

Have any of you ever tasted cranberries? How were they fixed? Did you like them? (It would be helpful to have some cranberries to show children plus some cranberry sauce for them to taste.)

Bridge

Cranberries play an important part in our story, *Cranberry Thanksgiving*. Maggie and her grandmother decide to invite someone poor and lonely to share their Thanksgiving dinner with them, but something unexpected happens during their dinner. Let's see what happens in Wende and Harry Devlin's beautiful book.

Discussion Questions

Significant Detail:
Did Maggie's grandmother like or dislike Mr. Whiskers? (She disliked him.) How do you know? (She shooed him away from their property whenever she baked cranberry bread because she was afraid he would steal her recipe; also, she didn't care for his appearance.)

Logical Deduction:
What did Maggie's grandmother mean by "Too many whiskers and not enough soap" when she talked about Mr. Whiskers? (She thought that his beard was too long and mangy, and he didn't bathe enough or wear clean enough clothes—these answers are all inferred.)

Significant Detail:
Why was grandmother so impressed with Mr. Horace? (He bowed, had a gold cane, and smelled fancy.)

Main Idea:
When Maggie said, "Grandmother! He's found it!" who did her Grandmother think had the recipe? (Mr. Whiskers.) Why? (Because she didn't trust him.)

Significant Detail:
Who really took the recipe? (Mr. Horace.)
Why did he want it? (For his restaurant in the city.)

Personal Relevance:
Have you ever had a wrong opinion of someone, based on how they looked? Tell about that time.

Personal Prophecy:
How do you think Grandmother will act toward people she meets in the future?

Personal Judgment:
Do you think it was kind or foolish for Maggie and her grandmother to let Mr. Horace come back for a piece of pumpkin pie? Explain why you feel that way.

Activities

Poetry:

In the story *Cinderella*, magic turns a pumpkin into a coach. Would it take magic to turn a pumpkin into a pie? Let's find out in "Thanksgiving Magic," by Rowena Bastin Bennett, from *The Random House Book of Poetry for Children*, page 46.

Cooking:

CRANBERRY THANKSGIVING BREAD

1. Turn on oven to 350°.
2. Measure into a large mixing bowl:
   2 cups flour
   1 cup sugar
   1½ teaspoons baking powder
   ½ teaspoon baking soda
   ½ teaspoon salt
   1 teaspoon grated orange peel
3. Add the following wet ingredients and turn mixer on slowly:
   ¾ cup orange juice
   2 tablespoons oil
4. Crack open 1 egg into a cup. Add to the mix and beat until smooth.
5. Add and stir in very gently:
   1 cup chopped cranberries
   ½ cup chopped walnuts
6. Use margarine to grease a 9½" × 5" loaf pan or two smaller pans.
7. Bake about 1 hour.

From *After the Story's Over: Your Enrichment Guide to 88 Read-Aloud Children's Classics*, published by Scott, Foresman and Company. Copyright © 1991 Linda K. Garrity.

Crow Boy

AUTHOR: Taro Yashima

ILLUSTRATOR: Taro Yashima

PUBLISHING INFORMATION:
Viking, 1955, LB, ISBN 0-670-24931-9
Penguin Puffin, 1976, PB, ISBN 0-14-050 172-X

SUGGESTED AGES: 6–Adult

TOPICS: Japanese Children
School
Self-concept

THEME: Ostracizing people is harmful to both the perpetrators and the victims.

Setting the Stage

Have you ever felt left out of a group or felt that others were making fun of you? How did you feel inside? Have you ever left someone out or laughed at them? How did you feel later? Why do people (grown-ups do this too, only more quietly) sometimes make fun of others?

Bridge

Crow Boy is the nickname of a little Japanese boy who lived long ago and was made fun of and left out. I wonder why the other children treated him that way? Let's find out by listening to Taro Yashima's story.

Discussion Questions

Personal Judgment:
This story is written about a school a long time ago in Japan. Modern schools in Japan are more like our schools. Do you think something similar could happen in your school?

Personal Relevance:
Chibi was always left alone during study time and play time (recess). What do you think is the loneliest time to be without a friend during the day?

Significant Detail:
What did Chibi do to occupy his time, since he could not learn his school lessons? (He stared at the ceiling, his desk, out the window. He also examined insects and listened for different sounds.)

Personal Relevance:
What do you do when you have difficulty doing a school paper?

Personal Prophecy:
If you had been one of the children listening to Chibi at the school program, how would you have felt?

Logical Deduction:
Do you think the story would have had a happy ending if Mr. Isobe had not come to teach at the school? (No.) Explain why you think that way. (He recognized Chibi's special talents and befriended him.)

Personal Prophecy:
If you had been the first teacher, what would you have done to make life better for Chibi?

Main Idea:
Why did Chibi nod and smile when the villagers called him "Crow Boy"? (They were acknowledging his special talents.)

Personal Judgment:
When would nicknames be a kind idea and when would they be hurtful?

Personal Relevance (for older children):
In the story the children graduated after going to school for six years. How long do you have to attend school? How many years do you think you need? Think of all the reasons you can why the children in Japan only went to school for six years.

Logical Deduction:
Chibi was smart, though he had great difficulty learning school work. Think of all the reasons why Chibi had such difficulty. (Note: This is a good opportunity for the adult to explain learning disabilities.)

Activities

Creative Discussion:

Are there children who are left alone during recess? Do they prefer to be alone or do they not have any friends? Think of all the ways children in the class could make everyone's playtime a happier time. This could become an ongoing class project.

Writing:

Write a modern-day story about a child similar to Chibi who goes to school in the United States. Think of why others would make fun of him or her. Write a happy ending!

Craft:

Illustrate Japanese symbols with a scene from the story. See Activity 16.

From *After the Story's Over: Your Enrichment Guide to 88 Read-Aloud Children's Classics,* published by Scott, Foresman and Company. Copyright © 1991 Linda K. Garrity.

Directions:

Choose a scene from *Crow Boy* to illustrate these Japanese symbols.

Love 愛	Happiness 幸福
Friendship 友達	Kindness 親切

Doctor DeSoto

AUTHOR: William Steig

ILLUSTRATOR: William Steig

PUBLISHING INFORMATION:
Farrar, Straus & Giroux, 1982, HB,
ISBN 0-374-31803-4
Scholastic, 1984, PB, ISBN 0-590-33304-6

SUGGESTED AGES: 7–9

TOPIC: Dental Health

THEME: "Don't get mad, get even."—John F. Kennedy

Setting the Stage

What do you do to cooperate when you go to the dentist?

Bridge

Not all patients help their dentists. Look at the mouse dentist, Dr. DeSoto, on the cover of our book. In the story a large, dangerous patient comes to visit. What do you think Dr. DeSoto will do? Let's read William Steig's book to find out.

Discussion Questions

Significant Details:
Tell some ways the DeSotos were able to fix the large animals' teeth. (Large animals sat on the floor; Dr. De Soto used a ladder and a hoist, and he wore rubbers on his feet.)

Why didn't they want to let the fox into their dental office at first? (He was a large animal, dangerous to mice.)

Why did they change their minds and let the fox in? (They felt sorry for the fox.)

Personal Prophecy:
Pretend you were either Dr. DeSoto or his wife. Would you have let the fox in? Why or why not?

Personal Judgment:
Do you think the DeSotos were good or poor dentists? Explain why you think that way.

Personal Prophecy:
The DeSotos faced a big problem when they talked about fixing the fox's gold tooth for him. Tell about some other ways they could have solved this problem.

Main Idea:
What did the DeSotos do to get even with the fox? (They glued his teeth together after fixing the cavity.)

Personal Prophecy:
What do you think will happen the next time a fox comes to Dr. DeSoto for help?

Personal Judgment:
Which do you think was a meaner thing for the fox to do: to eat the DeSotos when he first came in the office or to eat them after they had fixed his bad tooth? Why?

Activities

Poetry:
Shel Silverstein's "The Crocodile's Toothache," from *Where the Sidewalk Ends*, page 66, also tells about an unusual dental patient with an unusual dentist. See if you can tell how the ending is different. These silly poems and stories make me glad to be a normal person who goes to a normal dentist!

Writing:
Provide newspapers and magazines for children to peruse for examples of advertising. Then have them create their own ads for Dr. DeSoto.

Craft:
Children can make a colorful dental health chart for home use. See Activity 17.

From *After the Story's Over: Your Enrichment Guide to 88 Read-Aloud Children's Classics*, published by Scott, Foresman and Company. Copyright © 1991 Linda K. Garrity.

Directions:

Color this Happy Hippo chart and put it on your bathroom mirror. Put an x in a square each time you brush and floss. Look in the mirror at the end of the week and see a brighter smile!

Brush and *floss* your teeth *every* day!

Sun.	Mon.	Tues.	Wed.	Thurs.	Fri.	Sat.

Morning

Night

The Doorbell Rang

AUTHOR: Pat Hutchins

ILLUSTRATOR: Pat Hutchins

PUBLISHING INFORMATION:
Greenwillow Books, 1986, HB,
ISBN 0-688-05251-7
Greenwillow Books, 1986, LB,
ISBN 0-688-05252-5
Greenwillow Books, 1989, PB,
ISBN 0-688-09234-9

SUGGESTED AGES: 5–7

TOPICS: Food
 Friends

THEME: It's a good idea to share with others.

Setting the Stage

Nearly everyone has had a parent give them a treat to eat, only to have a friend come for a visit at just that time. It's a problem situation everyone has faced. What do you do? Do you go on eating the treat in front of the other child, put the treat back and eat it later, share what you have with the friend, or try to get more for the other child?

Bridge

Today, we have a funny story about two children, Sam and Victoria, who face that same problem. Let's see how they solve it in *The Doorbell Rang*, by Pat Hutchins.

Discussion Questions

Main Idea:
How did Sam and Victoria solve the problem of eating a treat when friends stopped in? (They shared each time with the other children.)

Personal Prophecy:
I imagine those freshly-baked cookies looked wonderful to Sam and Victoria! Pretend you were either Sam or Victoria. How would you have solved the problem?

Logical Deduction:
Judging by how they solved the cookie problem, how would you describe Sam and Victoria? (Generous and kind or maybe foolish, depending on background and experiences.)

Significant Detail:
What was the children's mother trying to do while all the neighborhood children kept coming in? (Scrub the floor) What was happening as she was doing this job? (The kids were tracking up the floor faster than the mother could clean it.)

Personal Relevance:
What would your mother have done in the same situation?

Personal Judgment:
How do you think most mothers would react? Would they be proud that their children were so generous, or angry that the other children were making extra work?

For Older Children

Significant Detail:
Show children the first double spread in the book. Who does Victoria look like? (Her mother.) In what ways are they alike? (They have the same features, and both have red hair.) Now show the children the next to last page. Who does the mother look like? (The Grandmother.)

Logical Deduction:
What color of hair do you think the grandmother had before her hair turned gray? (Red.)

Personal Relevance:
Children often look like their parents. Sometimes they look like other relatives. Grown-ups like to point out features that cause their children to look

like one person or another. Sometimes children like this comparison. Sometimes it annoys them because they have heard it so often. How do you feel about being compared to someone else?

It is different for adopted children and stepchildren, because they often do not look like their parents. How would you feel if you were adopted and someone asked you who you looked like? (Often adoptive children like to discuss their feelings in a supportive situation. This discussion should help to increase the sensitivity of the other children on this issue. However, the discussion should not make them feel "on the spot".)

Logical Deduction:
Where do you think Sam and Victoria learned to be so generous and easy-going? (From their mother.) Where do you think their mother learned to be so generous and easy-going? (From the grandmother.) Why do you think that? (The mother was kind to her children and their friends, and in the end the grandmother was also kind to the group. Personal experiences could be used to answer the question also.)

Activities

Most families have special recipes that have been handed down from one generation to another. Sometimes these recipes are simple; sometime they are very complicated. Compiling a class recipe book could be an enriching activity for children. The project would not be too difficult if children have access to a photocopy machine and volunteers to type the recipes. The booklets could be taken home as gifts for Mother's Day or Father's Day or other family occasions.

The activity pages can be used with various age groups. The math cookie chart can be done with manipulatives for those needing visual assistance. See Activities 18 and 19.

Cooking:
Grandma's cookie recipe makes lots of delicious over-sized cookies.

GRANDMA'S JUMBO CHOCOLATE CHIP COOKIES
1. Turn on oven to 350°.
2. Mix with an electric mixer until creamy and smooth:
   2 sticks margarine
   1 cup brown sugar
   1 cup white sugar
3. Crack 3 eggs into a cup. Pour into mix and beat until smooth.
4. Add:
   ½ teaspoon salt
   1 teaspoon cinnamon
   1 teaspoon baking soda
   1 teaspoon baking powder
   1 teaspoon vanilla
5. Scoop 2 cups of flour into a large measuring cup. Slowly add flour to the mixture.
6. Now stop the mixer and remove beaters. (Don't lift out the beaters with the mixer on, or you'll have a mess!)
7. Use the flour measuring cup to measure out:
   2 cups oatmeal
   Stir into mixture.
8. Extras: Add either
   1 large bag chocolate chips
   1 cup chopped pecans
            or
   1 cup raisins
   1 cup chopped walnuts
9. For jumbo cookies use a ¼ measuring cup to scoop up dough. Level it off with your finger and then drop the dough onto the cookie sheet. Flatten dough with a spatula. Leave plenty of space around cookies.
10. Bake 8–9 minutes. Makes 2 dozen jumbo cookies.
11. Remove very carefully from cookie sheet to cool.

Grandma's Giant Cookie

Directions:

Circle the cookie that matches the one in each box.

Color the chips with dots inside *brown*.
You will find out what everyone says when
they eat Grandma's cookies.

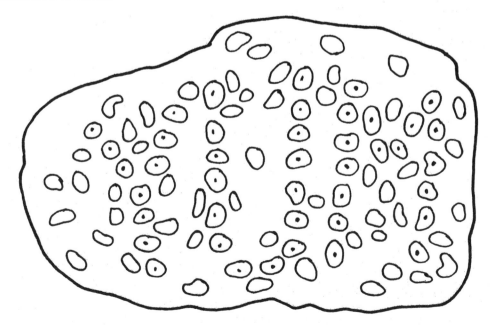

From *After the Story's Over: Your Enrichment Guide to 88 Read-Aloud Children's Classics*, published by Scott, Foresman and Company. Copyright © 1991 Linda K. Garrity.

Directions:

Each time additional children came to visit Sam and Victoria, it meant a
redistribution of cookies. Write in the numbers or draw the cookies in this
chart to show the changes in each child's share of cookies as more
children arrived.

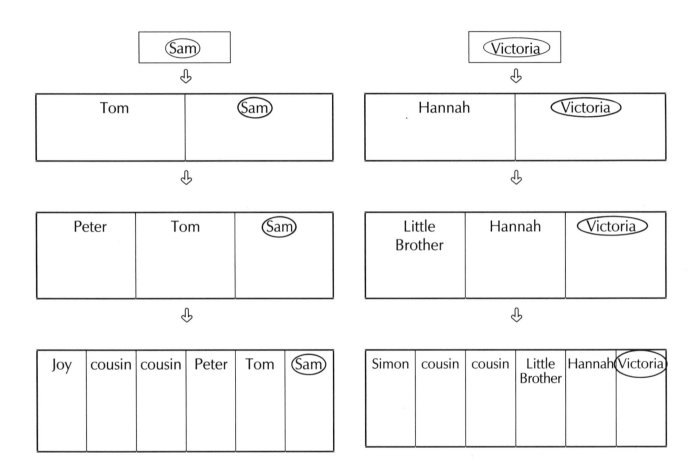

What would have happened if more children had arrived rather than Grandma?

The Duchess Bakes a Cake

AUTHOR: Virginia Kahl

ILLUSTRATOR: Virginia Kahl

PUBLISHING INFORMATION:
Scribner's, 1955, HB, currently out of print

SUGGESTED AGES: 6–8

TOPIC: Food

THEME: Follow recipes carefully!

Setting the Stage

Have you ever helped bake bread? What ingredient was put in the dough to make the dough rise? (Since most children will not know that a small amount of yeast is needed to make bread rise, perhaps the adult could open a packet of yeast. Tell them about this small, but important ingredient. Some bread mixes, however, already contain yeast.)

Bridge

Today's book, *The Duchess Bakes a Cake* by Virginia Kahl, is a rhyming story about a duchess who bakes an unusual cake. What do you think may be wrong with this cake? Why do you think it may have turned out that way? Let's find out!

Discussion Questions

Significant Detail:
Why did the Duchess decide to bake a cake? (She was bored; she wanted to surprise the family.)

Main Idea:
Why did the cake rise so high in the air? (She added six times too much yeast.)

Logical Deductions:
Do you think all the ingredients that the queen added were in the recipe? (No.) Why not? (They are not very sensible ingredients for a cake, and it says she put in whatever she found.)

Do you think the queen did much baking? (No.) Why not? (She wouldn't have added all those ingredients if she had had more experience.)

Personal Relevance:
Would you have enjoyed eating some of the Duchess's cake? Why or why not?

Activities

Poetry:
Here is a funny poem—"Peanut-Butter Sandwich," by Shel Silverstein, from *Where the Sidewalk Ends*, pages 84–86. It is like our story in several ways. It's nearly as long as our story!

Writing:
Pretend that you are the Duchess. Make up a recipe for a favorite food. Add a magic ingredient. Be sure to tell what it will do.

Reread the page where the Duchess describes her ingredients. This can become a game much like the old baby shower game, where a list is read aloud and at a given signal each person tries to jot down as many items on the list as he or she can remember. Since the list of foods is quite lengthy, the game could have several rounds.

Younger children might write down what they would purchase to bake a cake. Older children could do the same, but the concluding discussion should lead to a realistic assessment of the basic ingredients in baked desserts. It's also interesting for them to look at the list of contents in commercially prepared baked goods and mixes.

Research:
Have a dictionary on hand or, in the case of older children, provide several dictionaries in which they can look up unknown ingredients in the Duchess's cake. Knowing the true meaning of the words makes the story even more comical.

Drama:
The quantity of dialogue plus the rhymed text make this story a good selection for choral reading.

From *After the Story's Over: Your Enrichment Guide to 88 Read-Aloud Children's Classics*, published by Scott, Foresman and Company. Copyright © 1991 Linda K. Garrity.

Cooking:

The cake recipe is my Grandmother Katie's and is indeed light and luscious. By using white cake and frosting, a variety of colorful decorations can be added.

LOVELY, LIGHT, LUSCIOUS, DELECTABLE CAKE

1. Cream together:
   1⅓ cups sugar
   ½ cup shortening
2. Add:
   4 egg whites (have an adult help you separate these)
   1 teaspoon salt
   2 teaspoons baking powder
   1 teaspoon vanilla
3. Measure:
   2 cups flour
   1 cup milk
   Take turns adding a little of each until both are mixed in.
4. Run the mixer for an additional 2–3 minutes at high speed
5. Fill cupcake papers ⅔ full. In a preheated oven, bake 12–14 minutes at 350°. Or lightly grease and flour a 13 × 9 inch pan, and bake 25–35 minutes at 350°.
6. Cool and frost.

ROYAL BUTTERCREAM FROSTING

1. Add to a medium-sized mixing bowl and beat until fluffy:
   1 stick softened margarine
   2 cups confectioner's sugar
   1 teaspoon vanilla
   1 tablespoon milk
2. If the frosting is too stiff to spread easily, add more milk.
3. Frost each cupcake. Then add colored sprinkles, nuts, or chocolate chips to decorate.

From *After the Story's Over: Your Enrichment Guide to 88 Read-Aloud Children's Classics*, published by Scott, Foresman and Company. Copyright © 1991 Linda K. Garrity.

The Ghost-Eye Tree

AUTHORS: Bill Martin, Jr., and John Archambault

ILLUSTRATOR: Ted Rand

PUBLISHING INFORMATION:
Holt, Rhinehart, & Winston, 1985, HB,
ISBN 0-8050-0208-1
Holt, Rhinehart, & Winston, 1988, PB,
ISBN 0-8050-0947-7

SUGGESTED AGES: 5–8

TOPICS: Fear of Dark
Fall
Halloween
Siblings

THEMES: Fear of the dark can cause the imagination to play tricks.

Setting the Stage

Have you ever been asked by your mother or father to go get something or do something in a place that you thought was dark and scary? What was it? (The adult might want to start this discussion with memories of errands to the upstairs, basement, or back yard in the dark.)

Bridge

A sister and her little brother were asked by their mother to go across town to get milk on a dark, windy night. They were afraid, especially of one place on their walk, the "ghost-eye tree." Let's see what happens in this exciting story by Bill Martin, Jr., and John Archambault.

Discussion Questions

Logical Deductions:
Do you think this story happened recently or a long time ago? (A long time ago.) Why? (Because they go directly to the farmer for milk rather than the store; also there is a large woodpile by the door and a kerosene lantern, and the children have freedom of movement after dark.)

Do you think the big sister was mean to the little brother or do you think she really loved him? (She loved him because she ran back to get his hat.)

Main Idea:
What do you think there was about the ghost-eye tree that scared the children so? (The moon shining through it or an animal's eyes combined with their fear and imagination.)

Logical Deduction:
Why do you think the little brother was so fond of his hat? (It gave him self-confidence.)

Personal Prophecy:
If you had been Ellie, would you have gone back for the hat for him?

Personal Relevance:
Ellie said that she would add water to the milk so their mother would not realize that they had spilled some of it. Have you ever helped yourself to certain foods without permission and then fixed things up so your mother wouldn't know? What did you do?

Personal Judgment:
The little boy hides when his mother wants him to get milk at night. Do you think that is the best way to handle the situation or do you think he should explain why he feels the way he does? Why do you think that is the more reasonable way?

Activities

Craft:
The torn-paper craft can be used with a wide age range. See Activity 20.

Children could design a map of the story with all of the places mentioned and the ghost-eye tree right in the center. They might want to add a spooky border around the map.

Directions:

Make a Ghost-Eye tree picture by tearing black construction paper in the shape of a spooky tree. Cut different shapes of eyes and glue them on the tree or add ghosts, witches, and bats to make a Halloween picture.

Gila Monsters Meet You at the Airport

AUTHOR: Marjorie Weinman Sharmat

ILLUSTRATOR: Byron Barton

PUBLISHING INFORMATION:
Macmillan, 1980, HB, ISBN 0-02-782450-0
Penguin Puffin, 1983, PB, ISBN 0-14-050430-3

SUGGESTED AGES: 6–9

TOPICS: Friends
Moving

THEMES: While children usually adjust well to moves, they find them a challenging experience.
Children often have very little idea about the various geographic regions of the United States.

Setting the Stage

Have you ever moved? Before you moved, what did you think the new place would be like? After you arrived at your new place, did you find that you had been right or wrong about it?

Bridge

Look at the cover of our story *Gila* (hee'-luh) *Monsters Meet You at the Airport*. Gila monsters are large, venomous lizards that live in the southwestern deserts of our country.

The boy on the airplane looks scared. I'd be afraid also, wouldn't you? Like many American children, this boy has to move. I wonder what these giant lizards have to do with his moving? Let's listen to this story by Marjorie Weinman Sharmat to figure out this mystery.

Discussion Questions

Significant Detail:
What was the boy's first idea when he learned his parents had planned a move? (He wanted to remain in New York City.)

Logical Deduction:
Why wouldn't it work for a child to remain behind in the old home or apartment after the rest of the family moved? (There would be no provisions for care, finances, supervision, and family interaction.)

Significant Detail:
Where did the boy get the idea that Gila monsters would meet him at the airport? (From his friend Seymour.)

Personal Relevance:
Have you ever been told something by another child that turned out to be wrong? What?

Significant Detail:
What strange ideas did the other boy have about life in the East? (He thought there were gangsters, five minute springs and summers, airplanes flying through bedrooms, people sitting on one another in subways, and alligators meeting you at the airport.)

Personal Prophecy:
If you were the mother or father of either boy, what would you have done to help him with his fears about moving?

Logical Deduction:
Do you think the boy was beginning to adjust to his move to the West? (Yes.) What makes you think that? (He saw children doing activities similar to those he had done back East, and he commented that Seymour didn't know much about "us Westerners.")

Activities

Research:
Older children might like to know more about other areas of the country. They could choose a state and research its climate, opportunities for recreation, geography, main cities, and so on. They could compare and contrast various aspects of their area with the one researched.

Writing:
With some adult help, older children could write a parody of the book, using exaggerated aspects of their locale. The parody could be a class project, with each child contributing an illustrated page.

A different, easier project would be to write a parody on only the positive or negative aspects of the children's locale.

Writing:
People on vacation usually send postcards to friends and relatives. Children could pretend that they are on a vacation and send postcards to a friend, telling about their vacation. See Activity 21.

From *After the Story's Over: Your Enrichment Guide to 88 Read-Aloud Children's Classics*, published by Scott, Foresman and Company. Copyright © 1991 Linda K. Garrity.

Directions:

Color the postcard to Seymour. Write a message on the back.

Write your own postcard on a separate sheet of paper. Draw a picture on the back and color it.

Gregory, the Terrible Eater

AUTHOR: Mitchell Sharmat

ILLUSTRATOR: Mitchell Sharmat

PUBLISHING INFORMATION:
Macmillan Four Winds, 1980, HB,
ISBN 0-02-782250-8
Scholastic, 1984, PB, ISBN 0-590-40250-1
Macmillan (Reading Rainbow), 1987, PB,
ISBN 0-02-688770-3

SUGGESTED AGES: 5–7

TOPICS: Eating Habits
　　　　　Food

THEME: A moderate, balanced diet is best.

Setting the Stage

What are your favorite foods? What foods do you dislike? Do your parents think you're a picky eater? Why?

Bridge

Goats eat grass, weeds, and grain, though they will also eat materials made out of plants such as paper and fabric. They also lick on metal objects to get needed minerals. For this reason people have often thought that goats would eat anything.

This little goat on the cover is named Gregory. Look at the thought bubbles. What is Gregory thinking? I wonder why he is called "the Terrible Eater." Let's read this story by Mitchell Sharmat and find out.

Discussion Question

Significant Details:
What kinds of food did Mother and Father Goat like to eat? (Old clothes and other rubbish.)

What kinds of food did Gregory like to eat? (Nutritious foods such as fruits, vegetables, eggs, and fish.)

What did Dr. Ram suggest that Mother and Father Goat do about Gregory's eating habits? (They should introduce approved food slowly.)

Personal Prophecy:
If you were Dr. Ram, what would you have suggested to Mother and Father Goat?

Personal Relevance:
How do you think parents should handle picky eaters?

Logical Deduction:
What did Mother Goat mean when she said that Gregory should "eat like a goat, but not like a pig"? (She meant that Gregory shoud not be greedy.)

Main Idea:
After Gregory ate too much junk, he got a stomach ache. So what did he finally decide to do? (He decided to compromise and have a moderate diet.)

Personal Relevance:
What would be a reasonable meal for boys and girls for breakfast? . . . lunch? . . . dinner? . . . snacks?

Logical Deduction:
What makes this story funny? (The foods that Gregory's parents want him to eat are the opposite of what real parents want their children to eat.)

Activities

Poetry:
Listen to this poem, "I'd Never Eat a Beet," by Jack Prelutsky, from *The New Kid on the Block*, pages 124–125. Decide which foods Gregory would like. What would his parents want him to eat?

Would Gregory's parents have approved of Twickham Tweer? You'll know once you've heard "Twickham Tweer," a zany poem by Jack Prelutsky, from *The Random House Book of Poetry for Children*, page 151!

From *After the Story's Over: Your Enrichment Guide to 88 Read-Aloud Children's Classics*, published by Scott, Foresman and Company. Copyright © 1991 Linda K. Garrity.

Craft:

Young children who understand the story will enjoy creating a food poster for Gregory. See Activity 22.

Writing:

Children can write and design menus for two imaginary restaurants. Perhaps one could be called Gregory's Restaurant and the other one Goat Cafe. This activity is both creative and fun for children to do.

Cooking:

Gregory would have enjoyed eating a nutritious snack necklace. By preparing Gregory's necklace recipe, children can improve their fine motor skills and learn about nutritious snacks at the same time.

GREGORY'S NECKLACE

1. Use 2 feet of a brightly colored thread. Tie one end to a pretzel so the food won't fall off.
2. Here are some ideas for foods to string together to make a necklace. (If the food you choose already has holes in it, you won't need a needle.)
   Cheerios
   Olive slices
   Pretzels
   Mini-bagels
   These foods need holes punched through them with plastic straws:
   Cheese
   Pepperoni
   Sliced hot dogs
   Slices of fruits & veggies
   Use a needle on your thread for these foods:
   Popcorn
   Grapes
   Raisins
3. Add your own ideas, but remember, they must be nutritious. No cookies, candies, or chips!
4. Tie your necklace together and put it on. Show your necklace to your friends and then . . . eat your jewelry!

Directions:

Cut pictures of foods from magazines and catalogues. Glue each picture in the correct section.

Gregory likes. . .	Gregory doesn't like. . . 

Harriet's Halloween Candy

AUTHOR: Nancy Carlson

ILLUSTRATOR: Nancy Carlson

PUBLISHING INFORMATION:
Carolroda, 1982, LB, ISBN 0-87614-182-3
Penguin Puffin, 1984, PB, ISBN 0-14-050465-6

SUGGESTED AGES: 5–7

TOPICS: Candy
Halloween

THEMES: Being greedy with candy can make you ill.
Sharing sweets with others can be difficult.

Setting the Stage

What do you do with Halloween candy after you have finished tricks or treating?

Bridge

What do you think Harriet, the dog-girl on the cover of our story, is doing? Look at all the treats she has! I wonder what she is going to do with all that candy? Let's listen to *Harriet's Halloween Candy* by Nancy Carlson to find out what she does.

Discussion Questions

Main Idea:
Why was Harriet upset at the end of the story? (She had eaten too many sweets and spoiled her appetite for dinner.)

Why did Harriet give the coconut candy to her little brother? (It was small, and she didn't care for coconut.)

Logical Deduction:
Harriet's mother was very proud of Harriet for sharing her treats with Walt. Did Harriet deserve that praise from her mother? (No.) Why do you feel that way? (She only shared because she was too sick to eat it herself.)

Personal Prophecy:
Have you ever taken credit for something that you didn't actually do? Tell about that time. How did it make you feel?

Personal Judgment:

Do you think Harriet will handle her candy treats differently or about the same way next Halloween? Why do you think so?

Activities

Cooking:
Here's a tasty alternative to sugary Halloween treats.

HARRIET'S HALLOWEEN CHEESE BALLS
1. Turn oven on to 375°.
2. Carefully grate 1 cup chedder cheese into a bowl (or use 4 oz. package of grated cheese).
3. Pour in 1 stick plus 2 tablespoons melted margarine
4. Stir in:
   1½ cups flour
   1 teaspoon onion or plain salt
   1½ cups Rice Krispie-type cereal
5. Mold into balls.
6. Place on a cookie sheet.
7. Bake for 13–15 minutes.

Craft:
Activity 23 is useful for both visual discrimination and counting.

Directions:

Find the items that are listed below.

5 suckers

6 apples

7 candy canes

8 doughnuts

9 candies

Harry and the Terrible Whatzit

AUTHOR: Dick Gackenbach

ILLUSTRATOR: Dick Gackenbach

PUBLISHING INFORMATION:
Houghton Mifflin, Clarion Books, 1978, HB,
ISBN 0-395-28795-2
Houghton Mifflin, Clarion Books, 1984, PB,
ISBN 0-89919-223-8

SUGGESTED AGES: 5–6

TOPICS: Fear of Dark
Monsters

THEME: Fear of dark places and monsters is a normal part of early childhood.

Setting the Stage

Is there a scary place in your home? Where is it?

Bridge

Harry, the little boy on the cover of our story, thought that the cellar or basement was a very scary place. Why do you suppose he was afraid of that place? Let's read and find out in Dick Gackenbach's *Harry and the Terrible Whatzit*.

Discussion Questions

Significant Detail:
Why was Harry so sure that a monster was in the cellar? (Because the cellar was dark and damp and it smelled.)

Logical Deduction:
Why wasn't Harry's mother afraid of the cellar? (She didn't believe there was a monster down there.)

Significant Detail:
Why did the Whatzit shrink? (Harry was no longer afraid of it.)

Logical Deduction:
Why did Harry go down into the cellar even though he was afraid? (He wanted to save his mother from the Whatzit.)

Personal Prophecy:
Would you go into a scary place to save your mother or father? What would you take along for a weapon?

Personal Judgment:
Do you think Harry's mother was glad that Harry was there to save her from Whatzits, or do you think that she didn't believe him? Why do you think that way?

Activities

Poetry:
Let's listen to Shel Silverstein's poem "The Worst," from *Where the Sidewalk Ends*, page 130, and see if you think Harry would have liked it.

Art:
Children could use dark finger paint to create a monster painting.

Use the clay recipe in *Patrick's Dinosaurs* to make clay for children to model and paint their own monsters.

Drama:
Individual children could act out the part of the story in which Harry goes down into the cellar and fights the Whatzit. They could use a small child's broom as a prop.

Helga's Dowry: A Troll Love Story

AUTHOR: Tomie DePaola

ILLUSTRATOR: Tomie DePaola

PUBLISHING INFORMATION:
Harcourt, Brace, Jovanovitch, 1977, HB,
ISBN 0-15-233701-6
Harcourt, Brace, Jovanovitch, 1977, PB,
ISBN 0-15-640010-3

SUGGESTED AGES: 7–9

TOPICS: Valentine's Day
Trolls

THEME: One should marry for love, not riches.

Setting the Stage

Does anyone know what a dowry is? Who can tell what a troll is? (These concepts need to be explained before the story is read.) Have you ever been to a wedding? What was it like?

Bridge

Today's funny story, *Helga's Dowry: A Troll Love Story*, is not a love story as we usually think of one. It's not at all sentimental, though it has a wedding in it. I wonder who gets married?

Discussion Questions

Logical Deductions:
Why did Helga hide her tail and put on high-heeled shoes when she went to the Land of People? (So people wouldn't know she was a Troll, and then she could trick them.)

Is this a realistic story or a make-believe one? (Make-believe.) What makes you think so? (Trolls and magic are make-believe.)

(Turn to the fourth page of the story.) Why do you think Helga is sitting under the bridge with the Troll King and those three goats? (She sat there to think and also the goats may have been the ones from the "Three Billy Goats Gruff" story, because Helga was, after all, a Troll.)

Significant Detail:
Helga sang a little tune,
"Some people are lazy, some people vain,
Some people are greedy, it's all Helga's gain!"
(The word *vain* may need defining.) Which people were lazy? (The farmwife.) Which people were vain? (The townspeople.) Which people were greedy? (The rich man.)

Personal Judgments:
Do you think it was wrong for Helga to try to trick people so she could earn her dowry, or do you think it was wrong for people to try to take advantage of Helga? Why do you think that?

In this country, we don't have dowries for young women who are getting married. It is, however, a very old custom or practice for the bride's family to pay for most of the costs of the wedding. The groom's family pays for some things, but not as much as the bride's family. Which of the following statements do you agree with?

"The custom of paying for wedding expenses is very old, so it would just cause confusion to start changing the idea now."

"The custom of paying for wedding expenses is not fair to women, so modern people should try to change it."

Main Idea:
Why did Helga decide not to marry Lars after she earned the large dowry? (He only loved her for money.)

Logical Deduction:
Look back at the pictures to see who was watching Helga during her struggle. (The Troll King.) Why do you think that, in the end, he wanted to marry her? (He had watched her and admired her cleverness and determination.)

Significant Detail:
Look at the last page. What troll bridal custom is different from modern weddings? (Troll brides wear green instead of white.)

Activities

Writing:

Use a describing word for the letters in each of the
main characters' names.

H	L	I	K	T
E	A	N	I	R
L	R	G	N	O
G	S	E	G	L
A				L
				S

Children can look through newspapers to get ideas
for headlines for the story. Here are some examples:

"Local Girl Marries Royalty in Green Ceremony"
"New Wrinkle Cream Proves Unbelievable!"

Hey, Al

AUTHOR: Arthur Yorinks

ILLUSTRATOR: Richard Egielski

PUBLISHING INFORMATION:
Farrar, Straus, & Giroux, 1986, HB,
ISBN 0-374-33060-3
Farrar, Straus, & Giroux, 1989, PB,
ISBN 0-374-42985-5

SUGGESTED AGES: 6–9

TOPICS: Fables
Self-concept

THEME: Be content with what you have.

Setting the Stage

Have you ever wanted to go someplace, and after you arrived, wished you were back home? Where did you go?

Bridge

That's just what happened to Al and his dog, Eddie. I wonder where they went and why they wanted to leave? Let's find out in *Hey, Al* by Arthur Yorinks.

Discussion Questions

Significant Details:
Why were Eddie and Al unhappy? (Their apartment was crowded, and they were always struggling.)

What was so special about the place the bird took them? (It had gorgeous surroundings, no work, and plenty to eat and drink.)

Why did they want to leave? (They were turning into birds.)

Personal Prophecy:
If you could change anything in this story, what would it be? Hint: You could probably make a lot of changes in the Paradise part of the story, as well as the ending.

Main Idea:
What lesson do you think Al and Eddie learned? (To be content with what they had.)

Logical Deduction:
Do you think Al and Eddie are going to live just as they did before, or are they going to make some changes? (Make some changes.) What? (They will paint their apartment, wear brighter clothes, and change their attitudes.)

Activities

Writing:
Proverbs fall into two categories: those that are simple statements, expressing a generally accepted fact; and those that are metaphors or expressions that say one thing and mean another. Write these examples on an overhead or blackboard and discuss them with the class:

Simple Statements
Work before play.
Honesty is the best policy.
Seeing is believing.
Waste not, want not.
Try to please everyone and you will please no one.
No one believes a liar.
One good turn deserves another.
Haste makes waste.
He who hesitates is lost.
Practice makes perfect.
Where there's a will, there's a way.

Metaphors
Misery loves company.
Silence is golden.
Don't count your chickens before they hatch.
The grass is always greener on the other side of the fence.
Birds of a feather flock together.
When the cat's away, the mice will play.
A watched pot never boils.
The early bird catches the worm.
Too many cooks spoil the broth.
Look before you leap.
Don't cry over spilt milk.

A bird in the hand is worth two in the bush.
An apple a day keeps the doctor away.
You can lead a horse to water, but you can't make him drink.

The story mentions two proverbs, or wise sayings:

"Ripe fruit soon spoils."
"Paradise lost is sometimes Heaven found."

Which category does each belong in?

Younger children could select a simple proverb and write a short story or fable to exemplify the proverb. Older children might enjoy comparing the literal meanings of the metaphorical proverbs with the commonly accepted meanings and then select one proverb for a writing project (this involves higher level thinking processes).

Craft:
Eight- and nine- year-olds can create beautiful birds or other animals. See Figure 5.

Figure 5 _____

Directions:

For Paper Quill Birds, you will need 1" × 12" strips of brightly colored construction paper, pencil, and glue.

1. Shape strips of paper to form the outline of the bird's body, head, wings, beak, and so on. Glue these parts together.

2. Roll one strip of paper at a time around a pencil. Remove the pencil and glue the end of the strip down.

3. Roll enough strips to fill the bird shape.

4. Once you have enough strips, start filling the outline form. Begin closest to the outline form. Glue around the edge of a rolled strip and attach the roll to the form or to the other rolls.

5. Curl other strips to make head feathers, wings and tail.

6. Hang your bird around the room.

The House on East 88th Street

AUTHOR: Bernard Waber

ILLUSTRATOR: Bernard Waber

PUBLISHING INFORMATION:
Houghton Mifflin, 1962, LB,
ISBN 0-395-18157-7
Houghton Mifflin Sandpiper, 1975, PB,
ISBN 0-395-19970-0

SUGGESTED AGES: 5–7

TOPICS: Crocodiles/Alligators
Pets

THEME: Families become very attached to their pets.

Setting the Stage

Have you ever had a pet that could do tricks? What did it do?

Bridge

In our story, *The House on East 88th Street*, the Primm family has an unusual pet. Look at the cover and tell me what you think the pet might be. Let's see if you are right about this very unusual pet.

Discussion Questions

Significant Detail:
What did Mrs. Primm do when she first discovered a crocodile in her bathtub? (She was too frightened to even scream.)

Personal Relevance:
What would your mother do if she found a crocodile in your bathtub?

Significant Detail:
How did Lyle become accepted by the Primms? (He did household tasks and performed tricks.)

Logical Deduction:
What was the "one problem" with Lyle? (He liked to eat Turkish caviar, which was very expensive.)

Personal Relevance:
What does your pet do that makes him special to your family?

Personal Judgment:
Do you think Mr. Valenti was an honest man who was just trying to make a living, or do you think he was a selfish man who was looking out only for himself? Explain why you feel that way about Mr. Valenti.

Personal Prophecy:
If you had been a part of the Primm family, would have let Mr. Valenti take Lyle away? What would you have done?

Logical Deductions:
At the end of the story we know Mr. Valenti is no longer going to continue his stage and screen career. What clues tell us that? (The letter is signed "Former" star of stage and screen; and, also, Lyle is back with his family.)

Mr. Valenti wrote that he was sick of crocodile tears. Crying "crocodile tears" means pretending to be upset. Do you think Lyle cried *real* crocodile tears or pretend ones? (Real ones.) Why do you think that? (He was sad to be away from his family.)

Activities

Craft:
The origami project is more appropriate for older children. It results in a puppet with which children enjoy playing. The adult needs to lead children carefully through the project, step-by-step. See Figure 6.

Drama:
This story is the first of a series of books about Lyle, the unique crocodile. Older children could read the books and act them out, using their puppets.

Cooking:
The recipe is simple enough for even the youngest child and will serve an entire class. It's quite rich but not as sweet as you might think.

From *After the Story's Over: Your Enrichment Guide to 88 Read-Aloud Children's Classics*, published by Scott, Foresman and Company. Copyright © 1991 Linda K. Garrity.

LYLE, LYLE CROCODILES

1. Mix together in a large bowl:
   1 can sweetened condensed milk (14 oz.)
   1 can limeade, thawed (6 oz.)
   1 large carton whipped topping (12 oz.)
   ¼ teaspoon green food coloring

2. Pour mixture into a 9″ × 13″ pan. Smooth with a spatula.
3. Freeze for 3 hours.
4. Score into as many pieces as needed. Cut thin red licorice whips into 1 inch strips for a mouth and add raisins for eyes for each Lyle piece!

Figure 6 _____

Directions:

For origami puppet of Lyle, you will need green art paper (not construction paper), glue, paint stirring stick from hardware store (or old ruler), hole punch, string, tack, and scrap paper for body and features.

1. Fold paper (9″ × 18″ or 9″ × 12″) in half.

2. Open up sheet, turn over and fold each half in half again, making a fan fold.

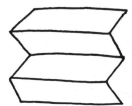

3. Place fan fold on table and open one flap.

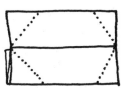

4. Fold all four corners into center. One set of corners will be triple thick.

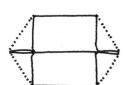

5. With corners folded in, fold back to original fan fold.

6. Make ½″ cut in center of long side.

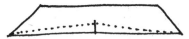

7. Fold from cut to end points on both sides. Open up. Will look like a beak.

8. Punch two holes in upper and lower lips. Put string through holes.

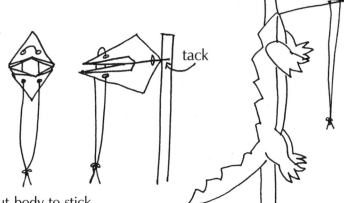

9. Attach head to stick with tack. Glue cut-out body to stick. Add eyes, teeth, and so on. Pull string to make mouth open and close.

From *After the Story's Over: Your Enrichment Guide to 88 Read-Aloud Children's Classics,* published by Scott, Foresman and Company. Copyright © 1991 Linda K. Garrity.

How My Parents Learned to Eat

AUTHOR: Ina R. Friedman

ILLUSTRATOR: Allen Say

PUBLISHING INFORMATION:
Houghton Mifflin, 1984, LB, ISBN 0-395-35379-3
Houghton Mifflin Sandpiper, 1987, PB,
ISBN 0-395-44235-4

SUGGESTED AGES: 7–9

TOPICS: Eating Habits
Families
Japanese Children

THEME: Cultural differences can be enriching for people.

Setting the Stage

Have you ever tried to eat Chinese or Japanese food with chopsticks? How did you do it? Do you think it is difficult using a knife and fork to cut up tough food like meat?

Bridge

Look at the title and the picture on the cover of today's story. What do you think might be the problem here? Let's read *How My Parents Learned to Eat* to find out if your ideas are correct.

Discussion Questions

Personal Judgment:
The little girl who tells the story is half Japanese and half American. Who would be some of the advantages? . . . disadvantages?

Personal Relevance:
America is a country of immigrants, and many people have a mixed parentage (parents and grand-parents of different nationalities and races). What is your parentage? What food or custom do you enjoy from that culture or cultures?

Significant Detail:
Why wasn't the uncle of much help to Aiko? (He taught her the British way of eating.)

Logical Deduction:
How do the British eat? (They hold the knife and fork in the opposite hands. A place setting of silverware would be helpful in this discussion.)

Main Idea:
Why do you think the parents wanted their daughter to learn to eat both ways? (They wanted her to appreciate and feel comfortable with both cultures.)

Personal Prophecy:
If you had been Aiko, would you have wanted to learn both the English and Japanese languages, as well as the different food and clothing customs? Why do you think that way?

Personal Judgment:
Frequently, American children of non-American parents lose much of their parents' culture when they grow up in this country. Do you think it's better for such children to try to fit into the American culture as much as possible, or do you think they should try to keep the language and customs of their parents' culture? Why do you think that?

Activities

Poetry:
"*Seymour Snorkle,*" by Jack Prelutsky, from *The New Kid on the Block*, page 118, is a funny poem about eating with chopsticks.

Eating peas presented quite a problem for Aiko. In the anonymous poem "I Eat My Peas with Honey," from *The Random House Book of Poetry for Children*, page 150, a rather unusual way of handling that problem is presented.

Craft:
Choose wrapping paper with a tiny print to make a lovely kimono. See Activity 24–25.

Directions:

To make a Japanese doll in a traditional kimono, you will need a tongue depressor and a sheet of 12″ × 18″ wrapping paper with a tiny print. Cut out the patterns and use them to trace the four kimono pieces onto the wrapping paper. Follow the directions in the numbered order on the patterns to fold and assemble the kimono.

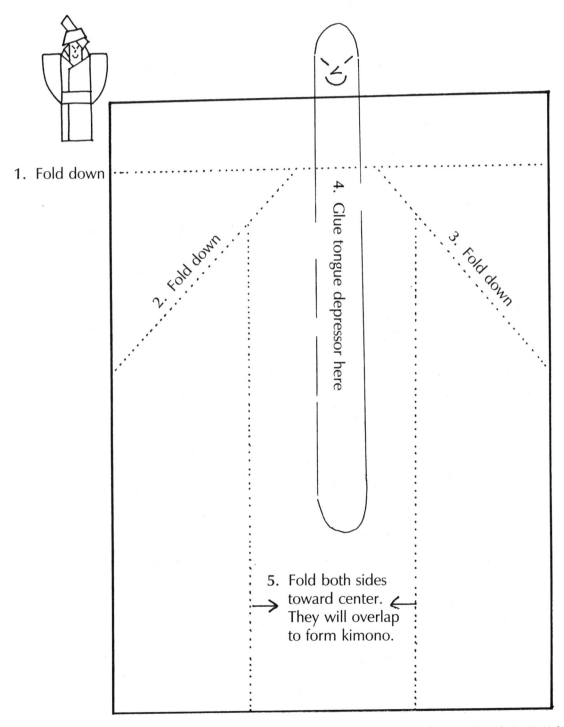

1. Fold down

2. Fold down

3. Fold down

4. Glue tongue depressor here

5. Fold both sides toward center. They will overlap to form kimono.

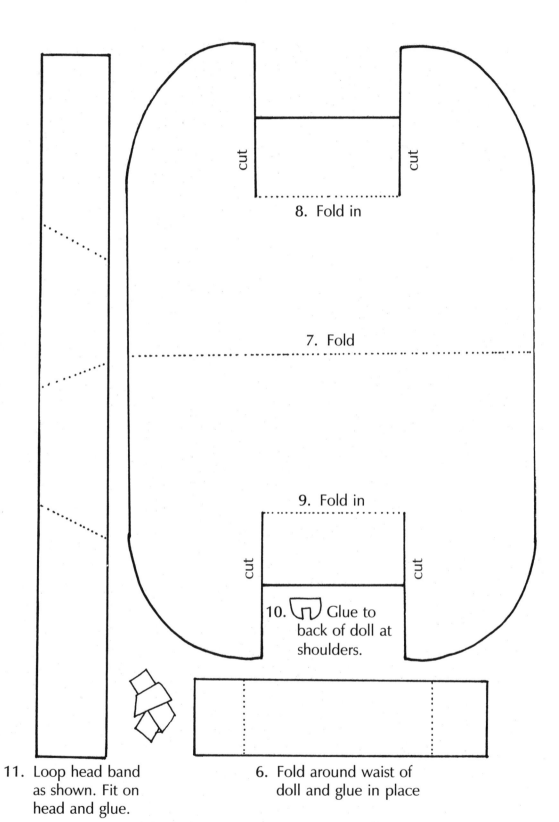

cut

cut

8. Fold in

7. Fold

9. Fold in

cut

cut

10. Glue to back of doll at shoulders.

11. Loop head band as shown. Fit on head and glue.

6. Fold around waist of doll and glue in place

Humbug Rabbit

AUTHOR: Lorna Balian

ILLUSTRATOR: Lorna Balian

PUBLISHING INFORMATION:
Abingdon, 1974, HB, ISBN 0-687-18046-5
Abingdon, 1974, LB, ISBN 0-687-37098-1

SUGGESTED AGES: 5–7

TOPICS: Easter
Rabbits

THEME: Even though it looks grim, a situation may turn out fine in the end.

Setting the Stage

Have any of you ever hunted for Easter eggs? Let's listen to different children tell us about exciting Easter egg hunts that they've had.

Bridge

In Lorna Balian's book, *Humbug Rabbit*, Granny planned a special Easter egg hunt for her grandchildren. It did not turn out the way Granny had planned. I wonder what might have happened? Let's listen to figure out this surprise. (The cover is unusual and greatly appeals to children. Call their attention to this and then make the book available for closer examination.)

Discussion Questions

Significant Detail:
Who told the rabbit children that their father was the Easter bunny? (Mouse.)

Main Idea:
What happened to make Easter a happy event for both the grandchildren and the Rabbit children? (Gracie, the cat, pushed Granny's eggs down the hole into the Rabbit family's burrow and that made the Rabbit children happy. After the chicks hatched, the rabbits took them outside, and the grandchildren played with the new chicks.)

Logical Deduction:
Easter eggs do not usually hatch into chicks. Why not? (Eggs must be kept warm by either the hen or an incubator in order to hatch. Also, Easter eggs are usually either hard-boiled or blown out.)

Personal Judgment:
What is your favorite character in the story? Why do you like that character best?

Personal Prophecy:
What if the cat had not pushed the eggs down the burrow? How would that have changed the ending?

Personal Judgment:
Decide whether it was a wise or foolish idea for the mouse to tell the Rabbit children that their father was the Easter bunny. Explain why you feel that way.

Personal Relevance:
Many children receive baby animals as Easter gifts. Have any of you ever received such a gift?

Personal Judgment:
What are some reasons why that may or may not be a good idea?

Activities

Drama:
An interesting pantomime could be enacted after the adult has read the story a couple of times. Cast members should be selected for two sections of the room for the two simultaneous settings. The adult should then slowly reread the story, indicating "above the ground" and "below the ground" for each scene.

Crafts:
After seeing the unusual illustrative layout in the book, children may be inspired to create a diorama of the Rabbit family home. Children could use two shoeboxes, stapled on top of each other, to create the effect of above and below ground.

Younger children enjoy making and manipulating the egg and chicken craft. See Activity 26.

Cooking:
The carrot bars are fairly nutritious as well as delicious.

GRANNY'S HUMBUG CARROT BARS
1. Turn on oven to 350°.
2. Mix together in an electric mixer:
   1½ cups sugar
   1 cup oil
3. Add 4 eggs and 1 teaspoon vanilla and beat well.
4. Add:
   1 teaspoon cinnamon
   ¼ teaspoon salt
   1 teaspoon baking powder
   1 teaspoon baking soda
5. Slowly stir in:
   2 cups flour
   2 cups shredded carrots
   ½ cup raisins
   ½ cup chopped pecans
6. Pour into a greased 9″ × 13″ pan and bake 25–30 minutes.
7. Cool.

GRANNY'S HUMBUG ICING
1. Mix together with an electric mixer until creamy and smooth:
   ½ stick soft margarine or butter
   2 3-oz. packages cream cheese (6 oz.)
   2 cups powdered sugar
   1 teaspoon vanilla
2. Carefully spread icing over the *cooled* carrot bars.
3. Cut into as many bars as needed.

From *After the Story's Over: Your Enrichment Guide to 88 Read-Aloud Children's Classics*, published by Scott, Foresman and Company. Copyright © 1991 Linda K. Garrity.

Directions:

1. Color and decorate egg.

2. Color chick. Glue onto backside of bottom half of egg.

3. Fasten two pieces of egg together with brass fastener.

Glue here

I Hate My Brother Harry

AUTHOR: Crescent Dragonwagon
ILLUSTRATOR: Dick Gackenbach
PUBLISHING INFORMATION:
Harper & Row, 1983, LB, ISBN 0-06-021758-8
Harper Trophy, 1989, PB, ISBN 0-06-443193-2

SUGGESTED AGES: 6–9
TOPICS: Food
Siblings
THEME: Sibling rivalry is a natural part of childhood.

Setting the Stage

Have you ever gotten *really* mad at your brother or sister? What did he or she do that made you so angry?

Bridge

Look at the cover of this story. Who do you think is angry? What do you suppose her brother has done to make her mad? Let's see what Harry has done in *I Hate My Brother Harry*.

Discussion Questions

Main Idea:
Why do you think the adults in the story do not mind the little girl expressing anger at her brother but do not want her saying that she hated him? (They felt it was natural to feel anger, but did not want her to confuse that with hatred.)

Personal Relevance:
How do the adults in your life react if you say that you hate someone, especially a brother or sister?

Logical Deduction:
Why do you think Harry was kind to his little sister when she was a baby, but not when she was a little girl? (Babies are cute and appealing, and they do not do things to annoy.)

Personal Judgment:
Do you think that an older child who has outgrown special toys should pass them on to a younger child to enjoy, or should the older child be allowed to keep the toys? Why do you feel that way?

Significant Detail:
What did Harry do to ruin his little sister's chocolate pudding? (He whispered to her that he had spit in it.)

Personal Prophecy:
If you had been one of the parents, how would you have handled this situation?

Personal Judgment:
Do you think Harry was really mean and cruel or just mischievous (ornery)? What is the difference between being genuinely cruel to a brother or sister and just teasing them?

Activities

Poetry:
Jack Prelutsky's "Mean Maxine, from *The New Kid on the Block*, page 66, is one of those poems with a twist to the ending. The poet has the same attitude toward Maxine that the little girl in our story had about Harry. Children could change the name "Maxine" to Harry and then make other changes throughout the poem so that it fits a boy instead of a girl and still rhymes. Or they could make up an entirely new and different poem about Harry.

Do you think Harry would agree with Prelutsky's poem "There is a Thing," from *The New Kid on the Block*, page 119.

Which person in our story would especially like Shel Silverstein's poem "For Sale," from *Where the Sidewalk Ends*, page 52? I'll read it again, substituting "brother" for "sister." Now who would like it?

Hating Harry must be a popular idea because here is a poem entitled "I Hate Harry," by Miriam Chaikin, from *The Random House Book of Poetry for Children*, page 104. Let's listen to discover what annoying thing Harry has done this time!

Writing:
Have older children rewrite an episode of the story, reversing the roles to big sister and little brother.

Craft:
Prepare older children for the portrait activity by discussing the average ages when people marry, have children, and become grandparents. While this varies greatly from family to family, children will still need some approximate ages to complete the family album. They can do the math by themselves, even if they count rather than add. See Activity 27.

Directions:

Draw Harry and his younger sister as they grow older.
Decide what their families might look like.
Figure out how old Harry and his sister will be in each picture.

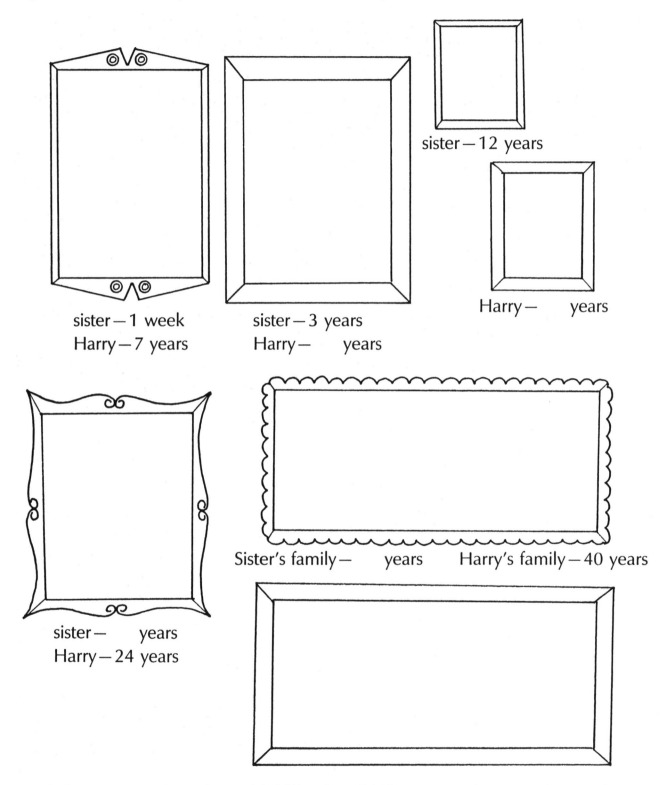

sister — 12 years

sister — 1 week
Harry — 7 years

sister — 3 years
Harry —   years

Harry —   years

Sister's family —   years   Harry's family — 40 years

sister —   years
Harry — 24 years

Ira Sleeps Over

AUTHOR: Bernard Waber

ILLUSTRATOR: Bernard Waber

PUBLISHING INFORMATION:
Houghton Mifflin, 1972, HB, ISBN 0-395-13893-0
Houghton Mifflin Sandpiper, 1975, PB,
ISBN 0-395-20503-4

SUGGESTED AGES: 5–8
(This story seems to strike a responsive chord in all ages.)

TOPICS: Friends
Teddy Bears

THEMES: Teddy bears can be a comfort to children. Avoiding embarrassment is important.

Setting the Stage

Have you ever stayed away from home overnight without your family? How did you feel after the lights were turned out and the room got quiet? (The adult should relate personal experiences of first separations, affirming the natural feelings of homesickness.)

Bridge

Sometimes a favorite stuffed animal can help children feel better when they have homesickness or do not like the dark. What does Ira, the little boy on the cover, have in his arms? Let's see how this teddy bear helps him in *Ira Sleeps Over* by Bernard Waber.

Discussion Questions

Significant Detail:
Who upset Ira about taking his teddy bear to his friend's house? (His sister.)

Logical Deduction:
Why do you think she tried to upset Ira throughout the story? (Maybe she was trying to help Ira or maybe she was trying to tease.)

Personal Relevance:
Do you have older brothers or sisters? Have they ever said or done something to tease you? What did they do?
   Do you have younger brothers or sisters? Have you ever said or done something to tease them? What did you do?

Logical Deduction:
Why do older children in a family sometimes enjoy teasing younger ones? (It makes them feel superior, a normal reaction.)

Personal Judgment:
Do you think teasing is ever an "okay" thing to do? Tell when it would be "okay" or acceptable. When is teasing a bad thing to do?

Main Idea:
When Reggie pulled a teddy bear out of his dresser drawer, were you really surprised? (No.) Why or why not? (He avoided talking about teddy bears when Ira kept bringing up the subject.)

Significant Detail:
What did Reggie and Ira plan for fun activities for their evening? (Making a junk collection, wrestling, having a pillow fight, doing magic tricks, playing checkers and dominoes, using a magnifying glass, and telling ghost stories.)

Personal Relevance:
If you have stayed overnight with a friend, what did you do for fun?

Logical Deduction:
(Hold up the picture on page 32.) Reggie's father has just said, "Bedtime!" to the boys. How do you think he feels? Why do you think he feels that way? (He feels exhausted. He is tired of listening to the boys' vigorous play and would like peace and quiet.)

Personal Relevance:
How do you usually feel about going to bed? How do you think your parents feel? Why might there be a difference?

Logical Deduction:
What do you think Ira's family thought when he came home for his teddy bear? (That he couldn't stand being away from his family for an overnight visit.)

From *After the Story's Over: Your Enrichment Guide to 88 Read-Aloud Children's Classics*, published by Scott, Foresman and Company. Copyright © 1991 Linda K. Garrity.

Main Ideas:

In the end why was Ira so sure that Reggie wouldn't laugh at his teddy bear? (Because Reggie had a teddy bear also.)

Why did both boys try to hide the fact that they slept with teddy bears? (They were afraid of being teased about them.)

Personal Judgment:

What do you think Ira will do the next time he is invited to sleep over at a friend's home? Why do you think that?

Activities

Poetry:

Boys often enjoy wrestling with their good friends, a fact that girls find very hard to understand. Kathleen Fraser tells all about this in "Wrestling," from *The Random House Book of Poetry for Children*, page 112.

Writing:

Children could write plans for a marvelous sleep-over. They could list activities and refreshments and even write a scary ghost story.

Janey

AUTHOR: Charlotte Zolotow

ILLUSTRATOR: Ronald Himler

PUBLISHING INFORMATION:
Harper & Row, 1973, LB, ISBN 0-06-026928-6
Harper & Row, 1973 HB, ISBN 0-06-026927-8

SUGGESTED AGES: 6–9

TOPICS: Friends
Moving

THEME: Adjusting to the loss of a best friend is very difficult.

Setting the Stage

Have you ever had a good friend move away? How did you feel after you realized that the friend was gone for good?

Bridge

The girl in this book by Charlotte Zolotow had a best friend named Janey. Sadly, the friend has moved away. How will this affect the girl? Let's listen and find out.

Discussion Questions

Personal Prophecy:
If you were the girl, what things would you do to make this difficult time a little easier?

Personal Judgment:
Do you think it is harder for grown-ups or for children to lose their best friends? Do you think it is harder for the child who is moving away or the child who is staying behind? Why do you feel that way?

Logical Deduction:
What can grown-ups do that children can't easily do to maintain friendships after someone has moved? (They can call long distance, write letters, and drive or fly to see their friends.)

Significant Detail:
The girl remembered ways that she and her friend were similar and ways that they were different. What were some ways in which the girls were similar? (They often said the same thing and called at nearly the same time; they both gave each other the same gift at Christmas.) In what ways were they different? (Janey liked to touch things rather than just look, and she was better at skipping rocks.)

Personal Relevance:
In what ways are you and your best friend similar? . . . different?
What would be most important to you in choosing a new friend?

Activities

Poetry:
Judith Viorst has written a beautiful poem that captures the very same feeling as *Janey*. See if you don't agree as you listen to "Since Hanna Moved Away," from *The Random House Book of Poetry for Children*, page 114.

Writing/Craft:
Children can make mailboxes and use the envelope pattern to stimulate letter-writing activities. See Activity 28 and Activity 29.

Directions:

Make a mailbox for you and your friends. Cover a half-gallon milk carton or shoebox with art paper or construction paper. Decorate like a mailbox. Put your name in large letters near the opening. Make sure the opening is at least 4″ wide.

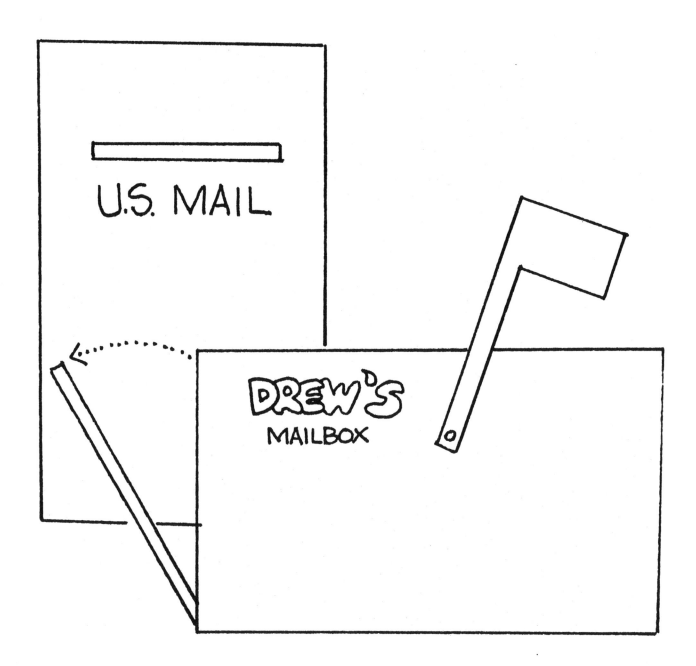

Directions:

Use the pattern to make your own friendship envelope for your letters.
Cut on solid line. Fold on dotted line. Glue. Decorate edges.

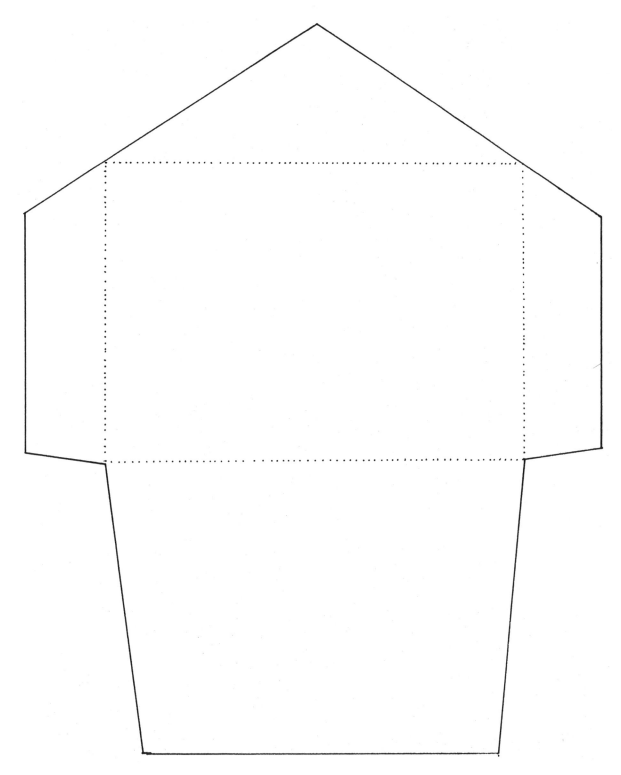

Jerome the Babysitter

AUTHOR: Eileen Christelow

ILLUSTRATOR: Eileen Christelow

PUBLISHING INFORMATION:
Clarion, 1985, HB, ISBN 0-89919-331-5
Clarion, 1987, PB, ISBN 0-89919-520-2

SUGGESTED AGES: 6–9

TOPICS: Babysitters
Crocodiles/Alligators

THEMES: Playing tricks on others can sometimes backfire.
Babysitting can be difficult.

Setting the Stage

What do you especially like about having a babysitter? What do you dislike about having a sitter?

Bridge

This is Jerome on the cover. He is getting ready for his first babysitting job. I wonder what kind of job he will have? Do you think those children in the picture will be easy or difficult to care for? Let's find out in *Jerome the Babysitter* by Eileen Christelow.

Discussion Questions

Logical Deductions:

Do you think Mrs. Gatorman realized how difficult her children were to babysit? (Yes.) What happened in the story to make you think that? (In the first part of the story, she rushed outside and pretended she didn't hear a loud crash. In the end when she returned home, she called her children "little devils.")

What do you think happened to Jerome's sister when she babysat for the Gatorman children? (They left her on the roof.) What makes you think that? (Mrs. Gatorman said that when Winifred babysat for her, she found her on the roof.)

Personal Prophecy:

If you had been Jerome, what would you have done to gain control of the Gatorman kids?

Personal Judgment:

Who do you think played the meaner trick: Winifred, when she tricked Jerome into babysitting the Gatorman kids; or Jerome, when he gave Winifred a box of frogs?

Personal Relevance:

Do you think babysitters enjoy taking care of the children in your family? Why or why not?

What could you do to make the babysitter's job a little easier?

Activities

Poetry:

Here is a funny poem to go with a funny story. It's called "The Sitter," from *A Light in the Attic*, page 14.

Listen to this poem by Jack Prelutsky—"Alligators Are Unfriendly," from *The New Kid on the Block*, page 14. Is it a better description of Jerome or the Gatorman children?

Craft:

Children can create a paper Jerome and the Gatorman children as well as the jumping frogs. They could use these figures to act out the story, if desired. See Activity 30 and Activity 31.

Writing:

Older children will see the humor in the following employment application for Jerome.

Employment Application

Position Wanted ___*babysitter for the Gatorman kids*_____

Name _____

(last)   (first)

Salary Expected _____ Date _____

Previous Experience _____

_____

References _____

Male ☐ Female ☐   Single ☐   Married ☐

Telephone Number _____

Special Talents _____

_____

_____

_____

Directions:

1. Fold 4″ × 11″ green construction paper in half in the direction of the arrow.

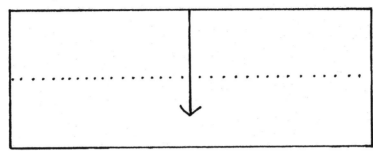

2. Draw an alligator using the folded edge for his back. Cut parallel slits along the fold.

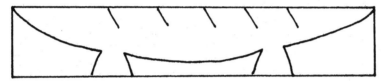

3. Unfold the paper and fold the slits backward. Fold the alligator in half again. Color an eye on both sides. Cut out teeth and toes.

Name _____

Activity 31

Directions:

You need: 3″ × 5″ green art paper or origami paper.

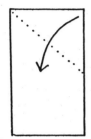 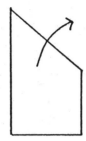 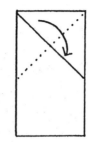 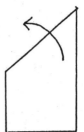

1. Fold down right top corner.

2. Unfold

3. Fold down left top corner.

4. Unfold

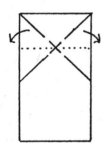 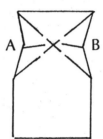

6. Unfold

5. Fold backward as shown by broken line, where lines cross.

7. Push down at X. Bring sides A and B to meet in the middle.

 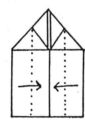 

12. Fold down top layer in direction of arrow.

8. Push down top triangle and crease sharply.

10. Fold sides of paper to the center.

11. Fold in half by bringing bottom edge up to the tip.

13. Stroke back of frog to make it jump!

9. Fold outer points up as shown.

 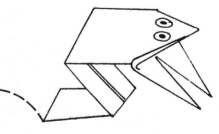

Jumanji

AUTHOR: Chris Van Allsburg

ILLUSTRATOR: Chris Van Allsburg

PUBLISHING INFORMATION:
Houghton Mifflin, 1981, HB, ISBN 0-395-30448-2

SUGGESTED AGES: 6–9

TOPICS: Animals
Imagination
Siblings

THEMES: You should read and follow directions carefully.
It can be important to complete what you start.

Setting the Stage

If you had the whole afternoon to play, what would you do?

Bridge

The girl on the cover of our story had the whole afternoon to play. Does it look like she's having fun? Let's read *Jumanji* by Chris Van Allsburg to find out what happened to her.

Discussion Questions

Logical Deduction:
Why do you think the game was especially designed for the bored and restless? (It was extremely exciting.)

Personal Relevance:
Which one of the jungle disasters do you think would have been the scariest?

Significant Detail:
What did Peter suggest that they do to solve the problem of the lion in the house? (Call the zoo or wait until their father returned.)

Personal Relevance:
What would you have done if a lion appeared in your home?

Personal Judgment:
After the adults came home, Peter told them truthfully what had happened. Did they believe him? (No.) Do you think adults usually want to know the complete truth, or do they usually want to know a "no-hassle" version? Why do you feel that way?

Logical Deduction:
Look at the last picture of the story. What do you think the Budwing brothers are taking home? (The Jumanji game.)

What do you think may happen? (They may have difficulties getting rid of the jungle disasters because they don't read directions or complete tasks.)

Main Idea:
What message does this story have? (You should read directions and finish what you start.)

Activities

Poetry:
Peter and Judy weren't the only children who spent an incredible afternoon. Listen to this boy's adventures in "True Story," by Shel Silverstein, from *Where the Sidewalk Ends*, page 43.

Craft:
Bring in some samples of postage stamps (maybe someone in the school has a collection that he or she would be willing to display). Then have children design a stamp to highlight a favorite scene from *Jumanji*.

Writing:
Explain the meaning of *sequel* to the class. Children could write an exciting sequel to *Jumanji*, featuring the Budwing brothers.

Older children could rewrite the story, using a different climate such as the polar region for the disastrous episodes.

Older children could create a crossword puzzle for this story. They need to make a list of possible words from the story, then fit them together for the grid, and lastly, write the clues to match the words.

Craft:
A Jumanji game could be created to match the story, using the gameboard base in Activity 32.

From *After the Story's Over: Your Enrichment Guide to 88 Read-Aloud Children's Classics*, published by Scott, Foresman and Company. Copyright © 1991 Linda K. Garrity.

Directions:

Design and color your own Jumanji game. You will need to add dangers along the path. You will also need a die or spinner and some pieces to move.

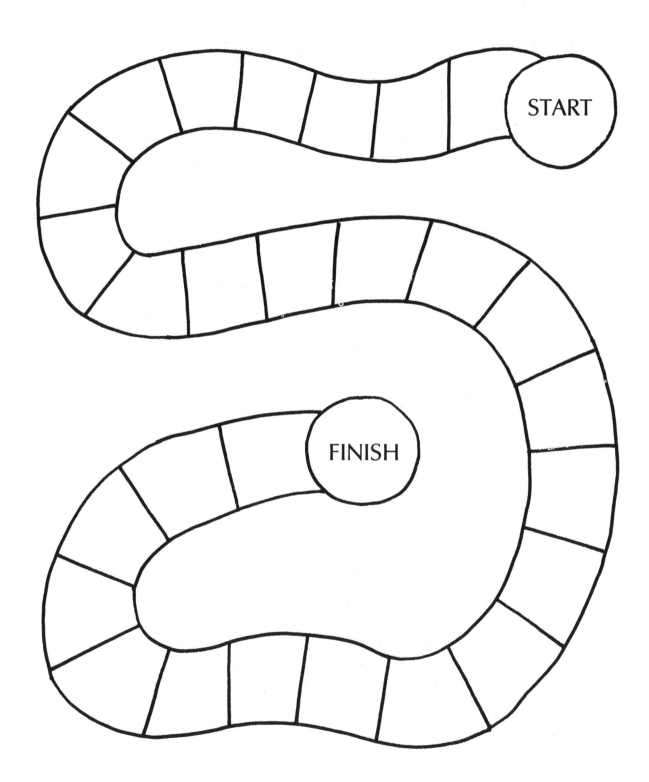

Leo the Late Bloomer

AUTHOR: Robert Kraus

ILLUSTRATOR: Robert Kraus

PUBLISHING INFORMATION:
Crowell, 1971, LB, ISBN 0-87807-043-5
Crowell, 1987, HB, ISBN 0-87807-042-7
Simon & Schuster, 1987, PB, ISBN 0-617-66271-6

SUGGESTED AGES: 5–8

TOPIC: Self-concept

THEME: Children develop at different rates.

Setting the Stage

Have you ever tried to do something such as play a game, draw pictures, or ride a bike, and you did very poorly at first? How did you feel when you saw others doing a better job than you?

Bridge

See the little tiger-boy on the cover of our story. How do you think he feels? It looks like he lives in a pretty place. Let's listen to *Leo the Late Bloomer* by Robert Kraus to find out why Leo feels so sad.

Discussion Questions

Significant Detail:
What were the things that Leo could not do well? (Read, write, draw, eat neatly, and talk.)

Personal Relevance:
We are all like Leo in that there are some things that are very difficult for us. I find it difficult to . . . (name several things). What is one thing that is difficult for you to do?

Logical Deduction:
Which parent was the most worried about Leo? (The father.) Why do you think he was more worried than the mother? (Maybe he didn't have as much faith in Leo as the mother, or maybe he had higher expectations.)

Personal Prophecy:
How would you have felt if you had been Leo and your father was watching you for signs of blooming?

Main Idea:
What do you think Leo's mother meant when she said "A watched bloomer doesn't bloom"? (Hovering over children does not help them develop more quickly.)

Personal Judgment:
What do you think Leo's parents could have done to have helped Leo bloom?

Personal Relevance:
Tell about one thing that your mother or father or teacher does that really helps you to learn.

Activities

Craft:
With careful guidance, older children can make beautiful tissue paper blooms. See Activity 33.

The "I Bloomed" pattern can come in handy all year long to congratulate children on their accomplishments. See Activity 34.

Directions:

To make tissue flowers you will need 8 pieces of tissue paper, cut 10" × 15". (You could use other sizes as long as they have rectangular dimensions. You will need a pipe cleaner for each flower.

1. Put all 8 pieces of tissue together. Pleat paper back and forth in 1" folds. Cut points or round each end after folding.

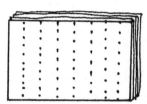

2. Twist a pipe cleaner around the middle of the pleated papers. Separate the top layer of paper. Make it stand upright by bunching it around the pipe cleaner. Do the same with each layer, always pulling paper gently toward the middle.

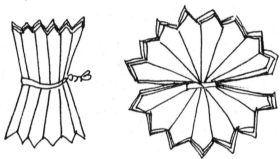

3. Push the twisted part of pipe cleaner inside a straw stem and glue on leaves if desired.

Name _____

Directions:

Fill in the information. Then color, cut out, and fold forward
on dotted lines. Wear your special bloom or pin it on a bulletin board!

_____ *Bloomed!*

I learned to _____

_____

Leprechauns Never Lie

AUTHOR: Lorna Balian

ILLUSTRATOR: Lorna Balian

PUBLISHING INFORMATION:
Abingdon, 1980, HB, ISBN 0-687-2137-1
Abingdon, 1980, LB, ISBN 0-687-21371-1

SUGGESTED AGES: 7–9

TOPICS: Grandmothers
St. Patrick's Day

THEME: It's better to do something constructive to help yourself than to do nothing and wish for magic.

Setting the Stage

When you think of leprechauns, what country do you think of? (Ireland.) What holiday do you think of? (St. Patrick's Day.)

Bridge

Look at the leprechaun on the cover of our book. What is he doing? Why?

Discussion Questions

Significant Detail:
What were Ninny Nanny and Gram's problems? (They needed to repair the thatch in the roof, gather potatoes for food, and gather firewood for warmth and cooking.)

Logical Deduction:
Why didn't they take care of these problems? (Ninny Nanny was too lazy and Gram was ill.)

In folktales the number three is important. Three different things happen, things happen three times, and sometimes there are only three characters. This story is written in the style of an Irish folktale. How is the number three used in the story? (Three problems, three similar solutions, and three characters.)

Significant Detail:
In keeping with the Irish flavor of the story, Lorna Balian used Irish-English words and expressions. Yet you were probably able to understand them. What gave you clues to the meaning? (Context.) What were some of those words or expressions and their meaning?

ailing—"ill or sick,"
naught but blathering between them—"they fought,"
agh—"oh" or "darn,"

is it raving you are?—"are you crazy?"
you've not the wit—"you're not smart enough,"
howled like a banshee—"shrieked,"
mite—"bit,"
Ninny Nanny—maybe "Nancy" or "noodlehead."

Personal Judgment:
Do you think it would have been a better or kinder idea for the leprechaun to have given Ninny Nanny the gold in the beginning or to have tricked her into doing all her own work? Why do you feel that way?

Main Idea:
What do you think Ninny Nanny learned by the end of the story? (That's it's better to do some work to improve your situation than to wish for gold.)

Personal Prophecy:
If you could change the ending, how would you have the story end? How would that affect the lesson that Ninny Nanny learned?

Activities

Poetry:
"The Search," by Shel Silverstein, from *Where the Sidewalk Ends*, page 166, is a poem about finding a pot of gold. Do you think the poet feels that finding the gold will solve all of his problems? Would the gold have solved all of Ninny Nanny's problems?

Stories about magic are fun to read. Another Silverstein poem—"Magic," from *Where the Sidewalk Ends*, page 11—describes most people's experiences with magic. See if you don't agree.

Craft:
Making the potato-head leprechaun is an unusual, comical activity. See Activity 35.

From *After the Story's Over: Your Enrichment Guide to 88 Read-Aloud Children's Classics*, published by Scott, Foresman and Company. Copyright © 1991 Linda K. Garrity.

Writing:

"Leprechauns" is a difficult word to spell. Children often use acrostics to help them remember how to spell words. For example, an old acrostic for *geography* is "George Elliot's old grandmother rode a pig home yesterday." The old acrostic for *arithmetic* is "A rat in the house may eat the ice cream." Help children develop acrostics for *leprechauns*.

Cooking:

There is a homemade butter recipe on page 146 to go with the soda bread.

IRISH SODA BREAD

1. Mix together in a large bowl:
   2 cups whole wheat flour
   1 cup white flour
   ½ cup brown sugar
   1 teaspoon baking powder
   1 teaspoon lemon peel
2. Add:
   1 beaten egg
   ½ cup oil
   1 pint buttermilk
   1 cup raisins (optional)
3. Pour into 2 well-greased 4" × 8" loaf pans.
4. Bake at 350° for about 45 minutes.
5. Empty onto racks to cool.

Directions:

Make your very own Leprechaun friend out of a potato. His hair really grows! Using straight pins, decorate a potato with button or construction paper eyes, ears, bow tie and pointed toe shoes. Cut out a small hole and stick in a carrot nose. Scoop out a 1″ hole in the top. Fill with potting soil and grass seed. Keep moist and see what happens.

Fold up

Fold up

The Little Engine That Could

AUTHOR: Watty Piper

ILLUSTRATOR: Watty Piper

PUBLISHING INFORMATION:
Many LB, HB, and PB editions available from several publishers.

SUGGESTED AGES: 5–6

TOPIC: Self-concept

THEME: Perseverance pays.

Setting the Stage

Have you ever tried really hard, for a long time, to learn to do something? What was it? How did you feel after you finally learned it?

Bridge

Something like that happened to the Little Blue Engine on the cover of our story. Let's listen to find out what he learned to do and how he felt about himself afterwards.

Discussion Questions

Significant Detail:
Why wouldn't some of the other engines help pull the train over the mountain? (The other engines were too fancy, too important, and too tired to help the train.)

Personal Relevance:
Have you ever been around people who acted like those engines? What did they say?

Significant Detail:
Why didn't the Little Blue Engine think he would be able to pull the train over the mountain? (He was too small and had never done that before.)

Main Idea:
How was the Little Blue Engine able to get the train over the mountain? (By trying very hard and saying, "I think I can.")

Logical Deduction:
How do you think the Little Blue Engine felt about himself after he got the train over the top? (He felt proud and happy.)

Personal Prophecy:
Pretend you are the Little Blue Engine. Chug your arms around and practice saying, "I think I can" a couple of times. Now think of other good things that you could say about yourself, like "I think I'm nice, I think I'm nice."

Personal Relevance:
What are some things that take children a long time to learn to do well? What are some things that grown-ups could do to help children to keep trying and not get discouraged (give up)?

Activities

Poetry:
"The Little Blue Engine," by Shel Silverstein, from *Where the Sidewalk Ends*, page 158, is a poem about our story. It has a different ending, though. After you listen to this poem, decide which ending you like best.

Game:
Children can play an interesting group game similar to Grandma's Trunk. The first player says, "The Little Engine that Could was pulling a boxcar full of apples." The second player says, "The Little Engine that Could was pulling a boxcar full of apples and balloons." The rest of the players follow, using other letters of the alphabet.

Craft:
The cut-and-paste "Over the Mountain" game is easy for young children to understand and play. See Activity 36.

Directions:

1. Color and cut out each engine.

2. Each player uses an engine as a marker.

3. Roll one die, move ahead the number of spaces shown.

4. First engine to reach the town wins.

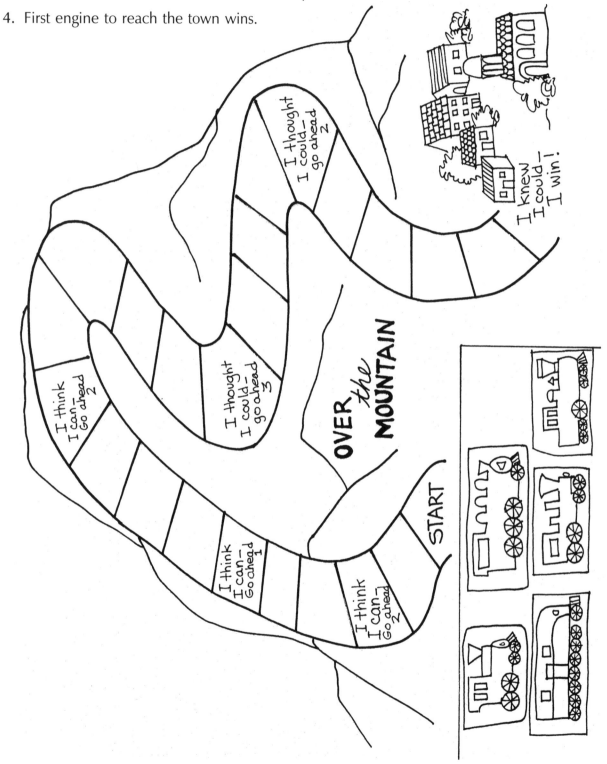

The Little House

AUTHOR: Virginia Lee Burton
ILLUSTRATOR: Virginia Lee Burton
PUBLISHING INFORMATION:
Houghton Mifflin, 1942, HB, ISBN 0-395-18156-9
Houghton Mifflin, 1978, PB, ISBN 0-395-25938-X

SUGGESTED AGES: 5–7
TOPICS: Environment
Seasons
THEME: Progress brings positive and negative changes to an area.

Setting the Stage

Give children background information (pictures would be very helpful) on what their locale looked like before it was developed.

Bridge

The Little House is an unusual story about the life of a small home. Boys and girls have for many years thought the pictures in this book were outstanding. Let's listen to find out what happens to this little house.

Discussion Questions

Personal Judgment:
How do the pictures in the story make you feel about the Little House?

Logical Deduction:
Each picture has a painting of the Little House. What else is the same about all the pictures in the book? (They have a rounded, circular design.)

Significant Detail:
What were the first changes for the Little House? (Cars and roads.)

Personal Prophecy:
(Show pages 7–10 again.) If you had been the Little House, which season would you have enjoyed the most? Why?

Main Idea:
How did the Little House feel about the city before all the changes came?

Personal Relevance:
Have you ever wished for something and then, when your wish came true, felt disappointed?

Personal Judgment:
People usually call the changes that happened to the area around the Little House "progress." Explain why you think progress is a good thing or why it is a bad thing.

Activities

Poetry:
"City, City," by Marci Ridlon, from *The Random House Book of Poetry for Children*, page 91, is a poem that talks about the good things and bad things about a city. Listen to both sections of the poem and decide which you think best describes a city.

Look at the picture of the Little House in the city at night. Think of that picture as you listen to this poem by Mary Britton Miller, "Where Are You Now?" from *The Random House Book of Poetry for Children*, page 98. Do you think the poem describes the city at night well?

The Little House also makes one think about the four seasons. Close your eyes as you listen to this poem, called "The Four Seasons," by Jack Prelutsky, from *The Random House Book of Poetry for Children*, page 35. Imagine playing outside during each season. Which is your favorite?

A short poem on the seasons that children enjoy memorizing is "Four Seasons," (Anonymous), from *The Random House Book of Poetry for Children*, page 36.

Look at the pictures of daytime, nighttime, and the four seasons (pages 3–13) in *The Little House*. What are the main colors of paint used in each picture? Colors remind us of different seasons and holidays. Hold up colored sheets of paper for the different holidays and seasons and have children try to identify the corresponding holiday or season. Start with Halloween—orange/black.

Craft:
The simple activity for the four seasons works well with children ages 5-7. See Activity 37.

From *After the Story's Over: Your Enrichment Guide to 88 Read-Aloud Children's Classics*, published by Scott, Foresman and Company. Copyright © 1991 Linda K. Garrity.

Directions:

Draw a little house and scenery for each season. Color the little houses
and the scenery.

SPRING   SUMMER

FALL   WINTER

From *After the Story's Over: Your Enrichment Guide to 88 Read-Aloud Children's Classics*, published by Scott, Foresman and Company. Copyright © 1991 Linda K. Garrity.

Little Rabbit's Loose Tooth

AUTHOR: Lucy Bate

ILLUSTRATOR: Diane De Groat

PUBLISHING INFORMATION:
Crown, 1975, LB, ISBN 0-517-52240-3
Crown, 1975, PB, ISBN 0-517-55122-5

SUGGESTED AGES: 5–7

TOPICS: Losing Teeth

THEME: Receiving money from the tooth fairy is the best part of losing teeth.

Setting the Stage

How many of you have ever lost a tooth? How many of you think you might have a loose tooth right now? Some children who have lost teeth might like to tell us how they lost their first tooth and what happened afterwards.

Bridge

Today's story, *Little Rabbit's Loose Tooth*, by Lucy Bate, is about a little rabbit girl who loses her first tooth. She thinks of many different things to do with her old tooth. What do you think she might do with her tooth? Let's discover what she finally does with it.

Discussion Questions

Significant Detail:
Little Rabbit thought of four different things to do with baby teeth after they've come out. What were they? Why didn't she like each idea? (Make a necklace—the tooth might break. Make a picture with stars—it might look silly. Buy candy with it—it's not really money. Throw it away—she didn't want to do that.)

Personal Prophecy:
If you lost a tooth, what new ideas could you think of?

Personal Relevance:
Name as many foods as you can think of that would be good for regular teeth. Now name as many foods as you can think of that would be good for loose teeth. How did you decide?

Logical Deductions:
Why did Little Rabbit's tooth come out in the chocolate ice cream? (It must have been quite loose.)

How did Father Rabbit feel about Little Rabbit's idea of what the tooth fairy does with baby teeth? (He didn't really believe in her idea.) What makes you think that? (He stammered around and did not answer her questions.)

Personal Prophecy:
If you were a tooth fairy and could put anything you wanted under children's pillows, what would you put there?

Personal Judgment:
Do you think Little Rabbit believed in the tooth fairy? Explain why you feel that way.

Activity

Craft:
The little tooth holders work quite well for holding teeth and coins. The tooth pattern and the bunny pattern give children an option for decoration. Younger children may need help cutting the slits. See Activity 38.

Name _____

Directions:

To make a Tooth Holder to put under your pillow, you will need
a piece of 3″ × 7″ felt (any color), 2″ × 2″ white felt, and glue.

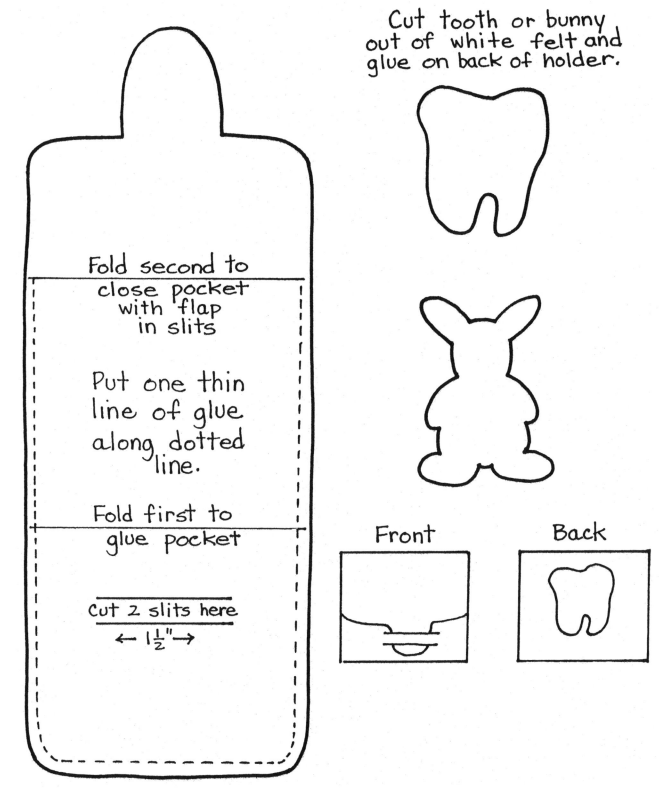

Cut tooth or bunny
out of white felt and
glue on back of holder.

Fold second to
close pocket
with flap
in slits

Put one thin
line of glue
along dotted
line.

Fold first to
glue pocket

Cut 2 slits here
← 1½″ →

Front

Back

The Lorax

AUTHOR: Dr. Seuss

ILLUSTRATOR: Dr. Seuss

PUBLISHING INFORMATION:
Random House, 1971, HB, ISBN 0-394-82337-0
Random House, 1971, LB, ISBN 0-394-92337-5

SUGGESTED AGES: 7–9

TOPIC: Environment

THEME: Lack of consideration for the environment will eventually destroy the quality of life.

Setting the Stage

What does *environmentalism* mean? (You may need to help children develop a definition.) How will the way people take care of the earth's air, water, land, and wildlife affect you by the time you're an adult?

Bridge

Today's story is by Dr. Seuss. Most of you have heard or read his stories before. What makes Dr. Seuss's books different from other books? (His books have made-up names and characters, are humorous and highly creative, are written in rhyming verse, and usually teach a lesson.) *The Lorax* has all those characteristics. I'm sure you'll know what the lesson is by the end of the story.

Discussion Questions

Main Idea:
What is the lesson in the story? (Failing to take care of the environment will eventually destroy the quality of life.)

Personal Relevance:
The Once-ler told the Lorax, "You poor stupid guy! You never can tell what some people will buy." Pet rocks were a fad for a time, and lots of people spent money on them. Can you think of other things that people buy that prove the Once-ler was right?

Logical Deduction:
Why did the removal of the Truffula Trees cause all the animals to go away? (The Bar-ba-loots no longer had shade and fruit. The smog from the factories forced out the Swomee-Swans, and the factory waste that flowed into the water forced out the Humming-Fish.)

Personal Judgment:
Dr. Seuss ends his story with hope, but the ending is not completely happy. Do you think the story would be more effective if Once-ler had not found the last Truffula Seed, giving the story a sadder ending, or if the boy had nurtured the Truffula Seed and rejuvenated the environment so everyone could return, giving the story a happy ending?

Activities

Writing/Drama:
The following project could be used as the basis for a panel discussion or a writing project.

Pretend you are a government official. People want to build a dam to create a large lake that will provide boating, fishing, and camping, plus thousands of jobs and water for farms and for drinking. The dam will also flood some ancient Indian ruins, unusual rock formations, and probably cause the extinction of a rare butterfly and one type of miniature chipmunk. What will you decide?

Explain to children that, before big projects such as dams and lakes and highways are started, the builders must give our government officials an Environmental Impact Study. This means that scientists study how the project will affect the air, water, birds, fish, animals, plants, and quality of life of people in the area. Then the government officials have to decide between the possible benefits (jobs for people and recreation facilities such as fishing, swimming, and camping) and possible harm to the environment.

The panel discussion could feature various scientists, farmers, boating and fishing enthusiasts, Army Corps of Engineers (who build dams to control flooding), environmental groups, unemployed

From *After the Story's Over: Your Enrichment Guide to 88 Read-Aloud Children's Classics*, published by Scott, Foresman and Company. Copyright © 1991 Linda K. Garrity.

people, archaeologists and geologists, plus children interested in camping and swimming. These groups could help the government officials make a wise decision.

Craft:

Children can draw before-and-after maps of the story, showing what the land looked like before the Once-ler came and after he had ruined it.

Writing:

Activity 39 is a comprehension word search. Here are the correct answers to Activity 39, with the correct words circled in the word search puzzle.

```
L E R S L O R C R U T U M B A R
T R U H W H F I F T U S W O M E
R L L E R K I N H U M C S N A I
U E O L B A F T R U F R W B W H
F R R L A S T R U F F U L A H L
U L A O R N E S W U T M T R I E
N O X R X P E N H N R M R B S R
L X O A S T N A I L U I X A W K
E C R I W H I I T E F E B L O B
C R H S O N T L R S T S A O M A
R W H U M M I N G S H W L O O X
U T H N E E D S T H N H N T N A
M S N A E L E T U M M I E S N A
M L E R K I R B A R S H E L X B
```

1. The Once-ler lives in a
   _____Lerkin_____ on top of his store.

2. The Once-ler will tell his story for
   _____fifteen_____ cents, a
   _____nail_____, and the
   _____shell_____ of a great-great-great
   grandfather _____snail_____.

3. The Once-ler talks in a
   _____Whisper_____-ma-phone.

4. In the days when the grass was still green,
   the _____Swomee_____-swans sang, and
   the _____Truffula_____-trees grew.

5. The Brown _____Bar-ba-loots_____ played in the
   shade.

6. The _____Humming_____-Fish splashed
   around.

7. Once-ler knitted _____Thneeds_____ out of the
   tufts of Truffula Trees.

8. The _____Lorax_____ spoke for the trees.

9. The Bar-ba-loots got sick with the
   _____crummies_____ and had gas in their
   _____tummies_____.

10. The Lorax left a small pile of rocks, with
    one word: _____UNLESS_____.

Directions:

Fill in the blanks and then find the words in the blanks in the word search puzzle.

L	E	R	S	L	O	R	C	R	U	T	U	M	B	A	R
T	R	U	H	W	H	F	I	F	T	U	S	W	O	M	E
R	L	L	E	R	K	I	N	H	U	M	C	S	N	A	I
U	E	O	L	B	A	F	T	R	U	F	R	W	B	W	H
F	R	R	L	A	S	T	R	U	F	F	U	L	A	H	L
U	L	A	O	R	N	E	S	W	U	T	M	T	R	I	E
N	O	X	R	X	P	E	N	H	N	R	M	R	B	S	R
L	X	O	A	S	T	N	A	I	L	U	I	X	A	W	K
E	C	R	I	W	H	I	I	T	E	F	E	B	L	O	B
C	R	H	S	O	N	T	L	R	S	T	S	A	O	M	A
R	W	H	U	M	M	I	N	G	S	H	W	L	O	O	X
U	T	H	N	E	E	D	S	T	H	N	H	N	T	N	A
M	S	N	A	E	L	E	T	U	M	M	I	E	S	N	A
M	L	E	R	K	I	R	B	A	R	S	H	E	L	X	B

1. The Once-ler lives in a _____ on top of his store.

2. The Once-ler will tell his story for _____ cents, a _____,

   and the _____ of a great-great-great grandfather _____.

3. The Once-ler talks in a _____-ma-phone.

4. In the days when the grass was still green, the _____-swans sang, and the

   _____-trees grew.

5. The Brown _____ played in the shade.

6. The _____-Fish splashed around.

7. Once-ler knitted _____ out of the tufts of Truffula Trees.

8. The _____ spoke for the trees.

9. The Bar-ba-loots got sick with the _____ and had gas in their

   _____.

10. The Lorax left a small pile of rocks, with one word: _____.

From *After the Story's Over: Your Enrichment Guide to 88 Read-Aloud Children's Classics*, published by Scott, Foresman and Company. Copyright © 1991 Linda K. Garrity.

Madeline

AUTHOR: Ludwig Bemelmans

ILLUSTRATOR: Ludwig Bemelmans

PUBLISHING INFORMATION:
Viking, 1958, HB, ISBN 0-670-44580-0
Penguin Puffin, 1977, PB, ISBN 0-14-050198-3

SUGGESTED AGES: 6–8

TOPIC: French Children

THEME: Children can become jealous when gifts and attention are bestowed upon a sick child.

Setting the Stage

Have you ever felt that other children got a little too much attention when they were sick? What was done for them or given to them?

Bridge

The other little girls in this story felt Madeline got too much attention when she had an operation. This story was written long ago about a group of little girls who lived in a boarding school in Paris, France. Their school life was very different from yours and different from school life for modern French children also. I wonder why Madeline needed an operation? I also wonder what life was like in Paris then? Let's find out in this story by Ludwig Bemelmans.

Discussion Questions

Significant Detail:
How was Madeline different from the other girls? (She was the smallest, bravest, and most mischievous.)

Personal Relevance:
Do you know any children who are rather like Madeline?

Personal Judgment:
How was Miss Clavel different from your teacher? How was she similar?

Personal Prophecy:
Do you think you would have enjoyed going to a boarding school like Madeline's? What would you have liked and disliked about it?

Logical Deduction:
Look at the picture with the nurse. How have hospitals and doctors changed? (Different uniforms and beds; use of paramedics for house calls.)

Main Idea:
Why were the other little girls upset after their hospital visit with Madeline? (They wanted toys, candy, and attention like that Madeline received.)

Personal Judgment:
Do you think most people would rather be well, or be sick and receive special treatment?

Activities

Writing/Drawing:
Children could tell or write a short piece, explaining, "When I am sick, I like (or don't like). . . ." They could also draw pictures to accompany their theme.

Writing:
Activity 40 is a simple letter-writing activity.

Craft:
Activity 41 is a pop-up Madeline greeting card that children can color, cut, and fill in.

Directions:

Reverse fold on the dotted line to make a get-well card for Madeline.
Color the picture and write a message inside.

Cut out along solid line.

Now make a get-well or friendship card for someone special that you know.

Directions:

Draw Madeline in bed. Then cut out the card around the dotted line.
Fold the card on the dashed lines to make Madeline's bed 3-dimensional.
Write a get-well message to Madeline on the lines.

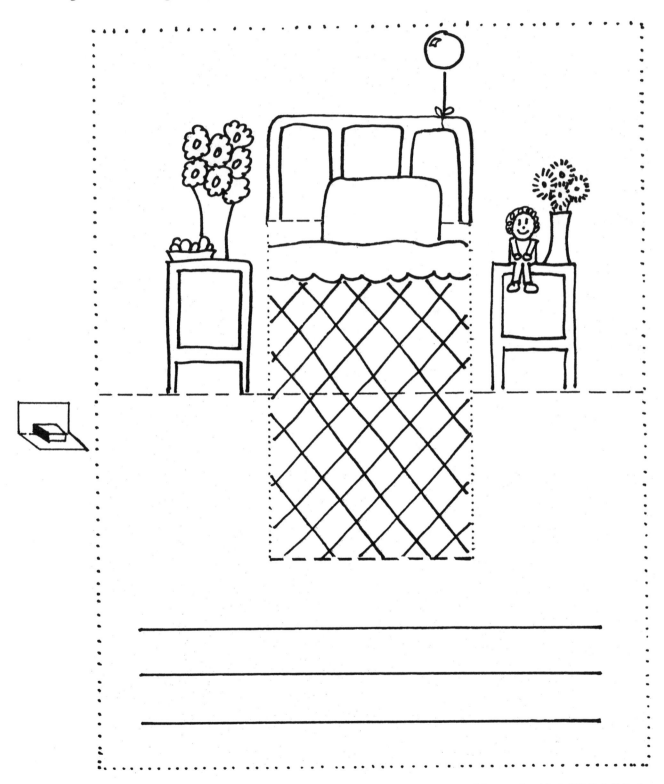

Miss Nelson Is Missing!

AUTHOR: Harry Allard

ILLUSTRATOR: James Marshall

PUBLISHING INFORMATION:
Houghton Mifflin, 1977, LB, ISBN 0-395-25296-2
Scholastic, 1978, PB, ISBN 0-590-11877-3
Houghton Mifflin, 1985, PB, ISBN 0-395-40146-1

SUGGESTED AGES: 5–8 (Five-year-olds enjoy this story, though they usually do not figure out the ending on their own.)

TOPIC: School

THEME: Sometimes teachers must use unusual techniques to gain control of their students' behavior.

Setting the Stage

Have you ever had a substitute teacher? What did he or she do different from what your regular teacher does? How did you feel when your regular teacher came back?

Bridge

In today's story, *Miss Nelson Is Missing* by Harry Allard, let's listen to find out what happens when a group of naughty children gets an unusual substitute teacher.

Discussion Questions

Significant Details:
What naughty things did the children in Room 207 do? (They threw spitballs and paper planes, whispered and giggled, squirmed and made faces, were rude during story hour, and always refused to do their lessons.)

What happened when Miss Viola Swamp took over the class? (She put the children to work, loaded them down with homework, and eliminated story hour.)

Main Idea:
Who was Miss Viola Swamp? (Miss Nelson.) What made you think that? (Black dress in closet, plus other small clues.)

Personal Relevance:
What helpful things have you done for substitute teachers?

Logical Deduction:
Do you think Detective McSmogg was a very smart detective? (No.) What did he do or say to make you think that? (When the children told him about Miss Nelson, all he could say was that she was missing.)

Personal Prophecy:
Pretend you are a substitute teacher. Think of all the things boys and girls could do to make your job easier.

Personal Judgment:
Decide if you thought Miss Nelson's way of controlling a wild class was a good one or not.

Activities

Drama:
Have a child enter the classroom, posing as Miss Nelson, then leave and return as Miss Viola Swamp. (An old wig as a prop would add to the fun.)

Craft:
Show pictures of the class on pages 9 and 29. If possible, either display a group picture (many schools have professional group pictures taken each year) or take a snapshot of the group. Then provide a strip of white butcher paper or several sheets of white paper taped together for each child to draw him or herself as part of a group portrait. (Adults need to draw themselves also!) The names of the individuals should be typed or printed in a key at the bottom of the portrait. Leave space for new children to add themselves to the group picture. Children might enjoy drawing themselves again, later in the year, to show changes in teeth, hair styles, and so on.

Miss Rumphius

AUTHOR: Barbara Cooney

ILLUSTRATOR: Barbara Cooney

PUBLISHING INFORMATION:
Viking, 1982, HB, ISBN 0-670-47958-6
Penguin Puffin, 1985, PB, ISBN 0-14-050539-3

SUGGESTED AGES: 7–9

TOPICS: Flowers, Self-concept

THEMES: We never know how, when, or if we will be able to accomplish our goals in life. Adding beauty to the world is a very worthwhile goal.

Setting the Stage

If you could live any place in the world when you grow up, where would you live? If you could do anything for entertainment or fun as a grown-up, what would you like to do? If you could do one thing to improve the world, what would that be?

Bridge

The older woman on the cover of our story had three goals in life when she was a young girl. They concerned the three questions that we just talked about. Let's listen to *Miss Rumphius* by Barbara Cooney to discover what her goals were and how and when she accomplished them.

Discussion Questions

Logical Deduction:
Why do you think the grandfather told Alice that she should do something to make the world more beautiful, rather than more happy or more fair? (He was an artist and saw that as an important value.)

Significant Detail:
What were the three things that Alice Rumphius wanted to do with her life? (Go to faraway places, live by the sea, and make the world more beautiful.)

Personal Prophecy:
She was not able to accomplish those things until later in life. What would be some creative ways that she could have accomplished those goals all at the same time or at an earlier period in her life?

Personal Judgment:
Miss Rumphius did not marry or have children. Do you think she would have been able to have accomplished her goals if she had had a family? Why do you feel that way?

Logical Deduction:
Why do you think Miss Rumphius's back stopped hurting? (She became excited and involved in the flower project.)

Personal Prophecy:
If you were the grandniece, what would be some ideas that you could try to make the world more beautiful?

Personal Judgment:
On the last page we see Miss Rumphius entertaining the neighborhood children with stories and refreshments. Do you think that adults who do not have their own children enjoy children more or less than people who have their own children? Why do you feel that way?

Activities

Interviews:
Have children interview adults about their goals for life that they held as children. Some interesting questions would be:
1. What were your goals and the ages at which you had those goals?
2. Which ones did you change or drop?
3. Why did you change or drop those goals?
4. Which goals did you reach?
5. Which goals are you still working on?
6. What helped you to reach your goals?
7. What harmed your efforts?

From *After the Story's Over: Your Enrichment Guide to 88 Read-Aloud Children's Classics*, published by Scott, Foresman and Company. Copyright © 1991 Linda K. Garrity.

Children should bring in results (no names) from several adults and tally or record their findings for a group discussion or essay on the factors that help or hinder goal attainment.

Writing:
An imaginary interview could take place at various times in Miss Rumphius's life. Some topics about which questions could be asked are age, profession, hobbies, accomplishments, goals in life, and favorite book or food. A picture of Miss Rumphius would also be a good idea.

Art:
Learning to paint lupines can teach children a simple watercolor or tempera technique that always gets excellent results. See Activity 42.

Gardening:
Children could plant packets of wild flower seeds in egg carton flower pots and try to identify the different varieties as they sprout and grow. The seedlings could later be planted on the school grounds or taken home.

Directions:

1. Draw three stem lines with pencil on white construction paper. Paint them light green.

2. Use violet, blue and pink paint and a small paint brush.

3. To paint lupine flowers to the stems simply press the side of the brush to the paper in dabs. 4–5 petals can be made with one dipping in the paint.

4. Greenery can be added but is not necessary.

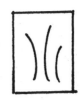

Molly's Pilgrim

AUTHOR: Barbara Cohen

ILLUSTRATOR: Michael J. Deraney

PUBLISHING INFORMATION:
Lothrop, 1983, HB, ISBN 0-688-02103-4
Lothrop, 1983, LB, ISBN 0-688-02104-2

SUGGESTED AGES: 7–9

TOPICS: Immigrants
Jewish Children
Self-concept
Thanksgiving

THEMES: Prejudice is an ugly aspect of society. Refugees continue to come to this country in search of religious freedom.

Setting the Stage

Have you ever heard children making fun of someone whom they thought was different? How did you feel about what they were doing?

Bridge

A group of girls at school made fun of this little girl Molly (on the cover) every day. I wonder why they did that? Let's see if we can find out in this true story, *Molly's Pilgrim*, by Barbara Cohen.

Discussion Questions

Personal Prophecy:
It is difficult for children to know what to do when they are ridiculed (cruelly teased). If you had been Molly, what would you have done to cope with the ridicule?

Logical Deduction:
Do you think this story took place in recent times or a long time ago? (A long time ago.) What clues make you think that? (The clothing and the classroom.)

Main Idea:
Why was Molly treated so meanly? (She was a Jewish immigrant.)

The theme of the story is readily apparent to adults, but not so obvious to children. For children growing up in multiracial communities, the theme will be more easily understood if an analogy is drawn between today's minorities and the Jews of a couple of generations past. Most children will be surprised to learn that Jews were discriminated against in this country. It should be pointed out that nearly all ethnic and religious groups have been the object of discrimination at some time or place in this country.

Personal Prophecy:
Miss Stickley was very kind to Molly and also very patient with Elizabeth's rude behavior. If you had been the teacher, how would you have handled the problem with Elizabeth and Molly?

Personal Relevance:
By now Molly and Elizabeth are probably grandmothers. Which older woman do you think you would enjoy as a next-door neighbor or friend? Why do you feel that way?

Significant Detail:
What did Miss Stickley say and do at the end of the story to make Molly feel happy? (She said that Pilgrims got the idea for Thanksgiving from Jews like Molly; she invited Molly's mother to school and placed the doll on permanent display on her desk.)

Logical Deduction:
Do you think life at school will now improve for Molly or will it stay about the same? (Either answer is acceptable.) What leads you to believe that? (Emma showed signs of friendship, but it might be difficult to change Elizabeth.)

Activities

Poetry:

Perhaps Miss Stickley would have liked reading Shel Silverstein's poem, "No Difference," from *Where the Sidewalk Ends*, p. 81, to her class. Listen and see if you can explain why.

Writing:

Boys and girls enjoy conducting interviews with their grandparents or other older relatives and/or friends. This project could be correlated with a letter-writing project, since many children do not live near a grandparent. See Activity 43.

The family tree project would coordinate well with the personal interview project. See Activity 44.

From *After the Story's Over: Your Enrichment Guide to 88 Read-Aloud Children's Classics*, published by Scott, Foresman and Company. Copyright © 1991 Linda K. Garrity.

When I Was a Youngster

Directions:

Choose an older friend or relative to interview. Ask the following questions. Write the answers on the lines.

Interviewer _____ Interviewee _____

When were you born? _____

What toys did you play with? _____

_____

Where did you live? _____

How many times did you move? _____

What did your room look like? _____

_____

How did you get to school? _____

Did you eat lunch at school or at home? _____

Who were your best friends? _____

What did you do at recess? _____

_____

What grade were you in when you had your first boyfriend/girlfriend? _____

Did you have a favorite teacher? _____ Why? _____

What singers and movie stars were popular? _____

_____

How did you and your friends dress when you were young? _____

_____

What kinds of cars were popular? _____

What sports were popular then? _____

What sports did you take part in? _____

_____

What other things were popular in your day? _____

_____

Directions:

Your parents will need to help you fill out your family tree, especially with the dates and the correct spellings of names. You may not be able to find all the information, but do the best you can. After this project is over, you may want to keep your family tree for future reference.

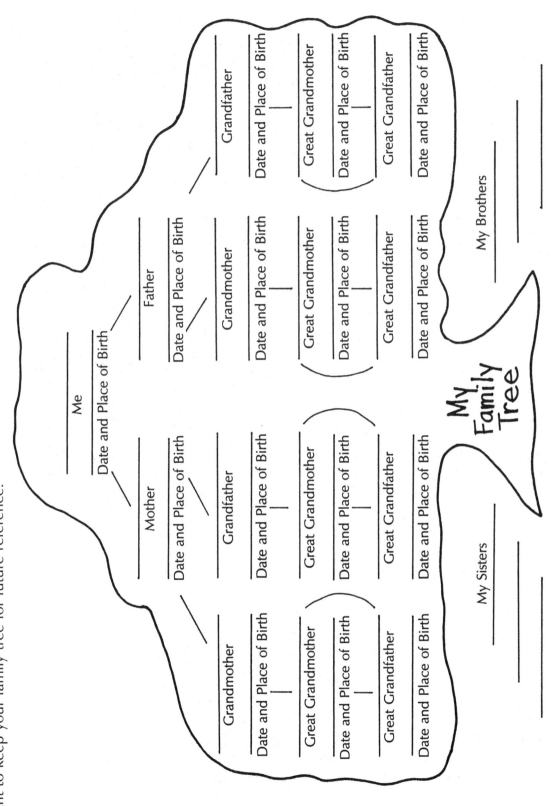

My Family Tree

My Friend John

AUTHOR: Charlotte Zolotow

ILLUSTRATOR: Ben Shecter

PUBLISHING INFORMATION:
Harper & Row, 1968, HB, ISBN 0-06-026947-2
Harper & Row, 1968, LB, ISBN 0-06-026948-0

SUGGESTED AGES: 6–8

TOPIC: Friends

THEME: Close friendships are a rewarding part of childhood.

Setting the Stage

When you spend time at a friend's home, do you notice differences in families and lifestyles (the way people live)? What things do you like about your friend's lifestyle? What things about your own lifestyle do you prefer?

Bridge

The two boys in today's story were best friends. Spending so much time together, they saw many differences and shared many personal parts of their lives with each other. They may be much like you in many ways. Let's read *My Friend John* by Charlotte Zolotow to see if you have ever felt like either of them.

Discussion Questions

Personal Relevance:
When you first go to someone else's place to play, what part of their home are you most curious about?

Logical Deductions:
The boy's parents and John's parents have different talents and also different rules. Why do you think families have such different rules? (They have different backgrounds and needs.)

What might be some reasons why John's mother does not want him to go out when the weather is bad? (He has poor health.) What might be some reasons the other mother doesn't care? (She might think fresh air is healthful, or she wants the boy out of the house.)

Significant Detail:
What were some of the private things that the boys shared only with each other? (Fear of dark, fear of cats, tears, and sweethearts.)

Personal Judgment:
Keeping a best friend's secrets is important. Yet, telling a best friend's secrets to an adult may sometimes be a wise decision. What kinds of secrets should you not tell? What kinds of secrets should you tell?

Logical Deduction:
Why were the boys so afraid of others knowing about their fears? (They feared others would laugh at them.)

Personal Judgment:
Do you think girls or boys hide their fears more? Why do you think that is true? Do you think it will change as you grow older?

Activities

Poetry:
Boys often relate to one another differently from the way that girls relate to one another. Kathleen Fraser's poem "Wrestling," from *The Random House Book of Poetry for Children*, page 112, tells about a part of some boys' friendship that many girls do not understand.

Writing:
When you grow up and have your own family, you can make the decisions about the way you choose to live. Write about the lifestyle you want as an adult. Include the number of children you want, your occupation, type of home and other possessions, the foods you will serve, types of recreation you will enjoy, rules for your family, and any other important parts of your family's life.

Writing/Craft:
Activity 45 can be drawn or written.

Directions:

Draw pictures in each box to illustrate the things that are alike and those
that are different about you and your best friend.

My family	_____'s family
My house	_____'s house
My favorite toy	_____'s favorite toy
What I'm good at ...	What _____'s good at ...

Draw more comparisons on a separate sheet of paper.

From *After the Story's Over: Your Enrichment Guide to 88 Read-Aloud Children's Classics,* published by Scott, Foresman and Company. Copyright © 1991 Linda K. Garrity.

My Teacher Sleeps in School

AUTHOR: Leatie Weiss

ILLUSTRATOR: Ellen Weiss

PUBLISHING INFORMATION:
Penguin Puffin, 1985, PB, ISBN 0-14-050559-8
Viking, 1986, HB, ISBN 0-670-81095-9

SUGGESTED AGES: 5–6

TOPIC: School

THEME: Sometimes young children do not realize that their teachers lead private lives away from school.

Setting the Stage

Girls and boys, here is a picture of a little girl/boy just about your age. Do you have any idea who this is? This is a picture of me taken years ago when I was _____.

My name was _____,
and I lived in _____
and attended _____.
Here is a current picture of me with my family/pets.
They are _____.
We live _____.

(Young children have many misconceptions about school and their teachers. This little story provides a warm, reassuring way for a teacher to take some of the mystery out of the school experience and provide children with a realistic portrait of the teacher as a private person. The teacher should preface this story by showing a collection of personal photographs—childhood pictures plus current family and home snapshots. Children are very curious about such exciting details as your first name, what your life was like when you were their age, your family, and where you live.)

Bridge

The children in today's story had a disagreement over where their teacher, Mrs. Marsh, spent the night. One little girl thought that the teacher slept in the school. Let's listen to *My Teacher Sleeps in School* to find out exactly where the teacher does sleep.

Discussion Questions

Significant Detail:
What led Mollie to think that her teacher slept in the classroom at night? (The teacher was always there, both when the children arrived and when they left.)

Personal Relevance:
I am always here when you come to school and when you leave. Why do you suppose that is so? (This can lead to an involved discussion, depending on how much the teacher wants to discuss the "work" aspect of teaching.)

Personal Judgment:
Which child would you prefer for a friend, Mollie or Gary? Why?

Personal Relevance:
Molly thought that teachers could do "anything." Do you think that is correct? Why? What are some things that grown-ups can do that look pretty amazing? Here are some things that children can do that seem amazing to me . . . What are some things that grown-ups can't do?

Personal Prophecy:
When the children went on their field trip to Mrs. Marsh's house, they did not know where they were going or what they were going to do. If you had been Mrs. Marsh, how would you have handled the trip? Why would you have done it that way?

Personal Relevance:
The children thought the school would be lonely and creepy at night. What do you think our school is like at night?

Logical Deductions:

How do you think Mrs. Marsh knew what the children were thinking about where she slept? (The note and the giggling, and the fact that she probably understood the children pretty well.)

Why did Mrs. Marsh save the biggest heart for Mollie? (Because Mollie was so sure that the teacher slept at school; maybe because Mollie was so thoughtful.)

Activities

School Tour:

Take the class on a tour of the "private" rooms of the school—teacher's lounge, boiler room, and so on. They are very curious about these "off-limits" places and feel privileged to see them.

Craft:

Young children can have a parent help them fill out "super stars." See Activity 46.

Directions:

Make a SUPER STAR for each child and adult in the class! Each star should be enlarged to fit an 18″ by 24″ sheet of heavy paper.

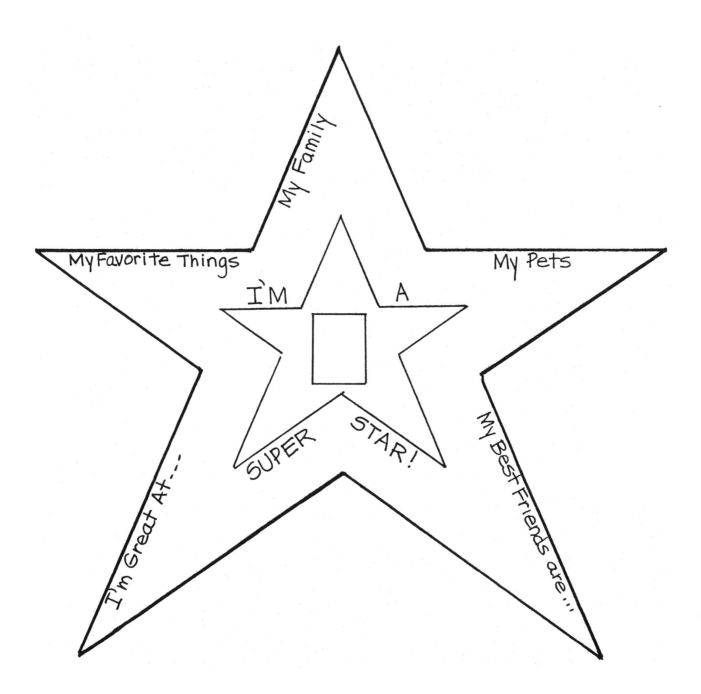

Nana Upstairs and Nana Downstairs

AUTHOR: Tomie DePaola

ILLUSTRATOR: Tomie DePaola

PUBLISHING INFORMATION:
Putnam, 1973, LB, ISBN 0-399-60787-0
Penguin Puffin, 1978, PB, ISBN 0-14-050290-4
Putnam, 1978, HB, ISBN 0-399-21427-8

SUGGESTED AGES: 7–9

TOPICS: Death
Grandmothers

THEMES: Death is a difficult but inescapable part of life. Relationships between grandparents and grandchildren can be very rewarding for both.

Setting the Stage

Most families have at least one relative who has a nickname. In our family . . . (the adult should relate some nicknames of family members and how they originated). Do you have people in your family with nicknames?

Bridge

Tommy, the little boy in our story, has nicknames for people in his family. Who do you think Nana Upstairs and Nana Downstairs might be? Let's see if your ideas are correct by reading this story by Tomie DePaola.

Discussion Questions

Significant Detail:
What did Tommy call his grandmothers? (Nana Upstairs and Nana Downstairs.) Why? (Because one was bedridden upstairs and the other one did lots of cooking downstairs.)

Significant Detail:
What did Tommy and Nana Upstairs do on Sunday afternoons? (Got tied into their chairs, ate candy, and talked.)

Personal Judgment:
Who do you think enjoyed the Sunday afternoon time more, Tommy or Nana Upstairs? Why?

Personal Relevance:
Do you do something special with a grandparent or other older person?

Significant Details:
Why did Tommy's older brother run away from Nana Upstairs? (With her hair down, she looked like a witch to him.)
What did Tommy think of her appearance? (He thought she was beautiful.)

Personal Judgment:
At 94 years of age the grandmother was probably not very glamorous, yet she looked lovely to Tommy. Why do you think he felt that way about her?

Significant Detail:
Eventually, what happened to Nana Upstairs? (She died.)

Main Idea:
Why do you think she died? (She was quite old; death was inevitable.)

Significant Details:
What did Tommy's mother tell him to help him understand Nana's death and feel better about it? (That his grandmother would live on in his memory.)
What did Tommy believe about his two grandmothers after they died? (That they were two falling stars in the sky.)

Logical Deduction:
(This is an advanced question.) What do you think Tommy meant when he said that he thought both grandmothers were now Nana Upstairs? (They were both now in heaven.)

From *After the Story's Over: Your Enrichment Guide to 88 Read-Aloud Children's Classics*, published by Scott, Foresman and Company. Copyright © 1991 Linda K. Garrity.

Activities

Poetry:

Who was the one person that really enjoyed Nana Upstairs' company? Older people often like children so much because children take time and care about them. A special poem by Shel Silverstein that talks about this situation is "The Little Boy and the Old Man," from *The Random House Book of Poetry for Children*, page 161.

Tommy thought Nana Upstairs' long white hair was lovely. In Rose Henderson's poem "Growing Old," from *The Random House Book of Poetry for Children*, page 159, we hear about another beloved grandmother with white hair.

Writing;

This story was written about a time long ago when older people stayed with their grown-up children when they were old and not able to take care of themselves. Where do many older people go now when they need care? (To nursing homes.) Why can't they stay with their children in many cases? (Often their adult children are working.)

Some older people in nursing homes do not have grandchildren and would appreciate letters and pictures from boys and girls. This could develop into an excellent letter-writing activity for children.

Now One Foot, Now the Other

AUTHOR: Tomie DePaola

ILLUSTRATOR: Tomie DePaola

PUBLISHING INFORMATION:
Putnam, 1981, HB, ISBN 0-399-20774-0
Putnam, 1981, PB, ISBN 0-399-20775-9

SUGGESTED AGES: 5–9

TOPICS: Grandfathers
Illness

THEME: The love and caring between a grandparent and grandchild flows both ways.

Setting the Stage

Many, perhaps most, children do not have loving grandparents who live nearby and spend time with them. If you are one of those lucky children who has a special grandparent, could you tell us about something happy that you have done together?

Bridge

Bobby, the little boy in our story, was one of those lucky children with a grandfather who loved him very much. His grandfather did many good things for him, and then one day Bobby had a chance to return the love and help. Let's see what Bobby was able to do in Tomie DePaola's *Now One Foot, Now the Other*.

Discussion Questions

Personal Relevance:
Like Bobby, everyone enjoys hearing stories about what they did when they were little. What is your favorite story about yourself?

Logical Deduction:
Do you think Bob would have recovered from his stroke without Bobby's help? (Probably not.) What makes you think that? (Bob was making no progress until Bobby started working with him.)

Discussion Questions for Older Children

Logical Discussion:
What is a stroke and why did it cause Bob so many difficulties? (Having some understanding of a stroke will help older children recognize the full meaning of the story.)

Explain to children that a stroke occurs when a blood vessel in the brain is clogged and breaks. Blood then flows into the brain and damages tissue. The consequences can be slight, with the patient recovering fairly quickly, or severe, with paralysis of part of the body. Some strokes even result in death. Most stroke victims need much physical therapy to help them recover.

Personal Judgment:
Who do you think did the greater service: Bob, because he loved and helped Bobby when he was little, or Bobby, because he loved and helped Bob when he was old and sick? Why do you think that way?

Personal Prophecy:
The title, *Now One Foot, Now the Other*, doesn't apply only to learning to walk. It could be used in other instances also. Think of a time when that saying could fit.

From *After the Story's Over: Your Enrichment Guide to 88 Read-Aloud Children's Classics*, published by Scott, Foresman and Company. Copyright © 1991 Linda K. Garrity.

Personal Relevance:

Most families have sayings that they use. Parents use them frequently. In my family . . . (Give an example from your family.) What are some sayings in your family?

Main Idea:

If you had to tell what this story was about in just *one* word, what would you say? (Love, caring, help, devotion.)

Activities

Poetry:

Who was the only person who noticed that Bob was responding? The poem ''The Little Boy and the Old Man,'' by Shel Silverstein, from *The Random House Book of Poetry for Children*, page 161, could be describing Bob and Bobby. Listen and see if you don't agree.

Writing:

Have children fill out the hospital chart about Bob's recovery. See Activity 47.

Name _____

Directions:

In the top part of the chart, describe the major changes in Bob's recovery. In the bottom part of the chart, mark points that indicate your opinion of Bob's progress. Use a ruler to connect the points, forming a graph of Bob's recovery.

Hospital Chart for Grandpa Bob

HOSPITAL

Patient has a stroke. Enters hospital.

Patient Behavior

Excellent

Poor

Patient Progress

Oh, Were They Ever Happy!

AUTHOR: Peter Spier

ILLUSTRATOR: Peter Spier

PUBLISHING INFORMATION:
Doubleday, 1978, HB, ISBN 0-385-13175-5
Doubleday, 1978, LB, ISBN 0-385-13176-3
Doubleday, 1988, PB, ISBN 0-385-24477-0

SUGGESTED AGES: 5–8

TOPIC: Houses

THEME: Sometimes children's help is more work than worth.

Setting the Stage

Have you ever tried to do something to help your mom or dad and it didn't turn out the way you had expected? Why didn't your help work out as you had wanted it to?

Bridge

In today's story the children decided to tackle a major job—housepainting—for their parents. Let's see what happened in Peter Spier's *Oh, Were They Ever Happy*!

Discussion Questions

Logical Deduction:
The title of the book is *Oh, Were They Ever Happy*! Do you think the parents were going to be happy when they came home? (No.) Then why did Mr. Spier give the book that title? (Because he meant just the opposite—the title has a double meaning.) Can you think of times when children and adults say one thing and mean the opposite?

Personal Prophecy:
If you were one of the parents, what would you say or do when you got home?

Logical Deductions:
Look at the last page. What do you think would be the most difficult parts of the house to repair or fix up? (Probably the windows, brick chimneys, and maybe walks and driveways.) Why would those parts be harder? (The wood can just be painted over, but these areas need to have the paint removed.)

Most parents do not let their children decide on paint colors for their rooms. Why do you think that is so? (They may worry that their children would choose too wild a color.)

Personal Judgment:
Who do you think was to blame for this mess—the parents, for not waiting until the babysitter arrived before leaving; the babysitter, for not showing up to care for the children; or the children, for not waiting until they had permission to tackle a big job like painting the house?

Logical Deduction:
Do you think this story could ever really happen? (Probably not.) Why do you think that way? (Someone would have said something to the children, because neighbors aren't afraid to question kids. The children look too old to be that unaware or foolish.)

Activities

Writing:
Show children real estate ads from the classified sections of the newspaper. Have them write an ad for the Noonan's home *before* the children's paint job. Then have them try to write a convincing ad *after* the paint job.

Craft:
Each child could use a large sheet of paper to design his or her dream room. Children should add labels for all appropriate furnishings and choose their favorite color scheme for decorating.

Old Mother Witch

AUTHOR: Carol Carrick

ILLUSTRATOR: Donald Carrick

PUBLISHING INFORMATION:
Clarion, 1975, HB, ISBN 0-395-28778-2
Clarion, 1989, PB, ISBN 0-395-51584-X

SUGGESTED AGES: 6–9

TOPIC: Halloween

THEMES: Taunting causes people to do things of which they're later ashamed.
Errors are made by judging others too hastily.

Setting the Stage

Have you ever had an opinion of someone and later changed your mind? What caused you to change your mind?

Bridge

What do you think the boys on the cover are doing? Does it look as if they're having fun? In this realistic Halloween story by Carol and Don Carrick their fun turns into a life-and-death situation because of David's opinion of his neighbor, Mrs. Oliver. Let's read *Old Mother Witch* to see why.

Discussion Questions

Significant Detail:
Why did the neighborhood children call Mrs. Oliver "old Mother Witch"? (She complained if they roller-skated in front of her house, chased dogs from her yard, wouldn't answer the door to David, scolded David when he retrieved a ball from her yard, and *possibly* poisoned Mary Ellen's cat.)

Personal Relevance:
Even though the boys knew it was Mrs. Bridwell in the witch's costume, they felt uneasy when they went up to her for candy treats. How do you feel around people in spooky costumes that are especially realistic?

Logical Deduction:
Did David want to go up to Mrs. Oliver's door? (No.) Why do you think he felt that way? (He was afraid.)

Main Idea:
Why did David finally go to Mrs. Oliver's door? (The other children dared him to do it, and he could not resist their taunts.)

Personal Relevance:
Have you ever been in a situation where another child or other children dared you to do something? How did you handle the situation?

Personal Prophecy:
If you had been David, what would you have done when you heard the other children ring the bell?

Personal Judgment:
What do you think most people do in group situations—go along with the crowd or stand up for themselves? In your opinion, what should you do? Why do you think so?

Logical Deductions:
How did David feel about himself after he played an important part in saving Mrs. Oliver's life? (He was probably glad that he saved her life, but ashamed that he had not done so under kindlier circumstances.)

How did Mrs. Oliver feel about David after she had recovered? (She was probably grateful to him for saving her life, but not comfortable enough to want to be friends.)

Personal Prophecy:
How do you think David would react to a new neighbor who seemed cranky or odd? Why? (He will probably wait to see what the neighbor is really like.) Why? (He had learned that we can easily make errors by judging others too hastily.)

Personal Relevance:

How do you think you may react to someone, young or old, who seems different or unfriendly?

Activities

Poetry:

A very moving poem that ends the way our story could have ended is "House, For Sale," by Leonard Clark, from *The Random House Book of Poetry for Children*, page 162.

Drama:

Have children turn the story into a legal trial. Select children to be a judge, Mrs. Oliver, an attorney for Mrs. Oliver, the various children and their attorney, and a jury. Mrs. Oliver is the plaintiff with a case of harassment against the neighborhood children. The judge and jury should be instructed to reach a final verdict and a solution to resolve the differences between the two parties. Children should find the case interesting.

From *After the Story's Over: Your Enrichment Guide to 88 Read-Aloud Children's Classics*, published by Scott, Foresman and Company. Copyright © 1991 Linda K. Garrity.

Ox-Cart Man

AUTHOR: Donald Hall

ILLUSTRATOR: Barbara Cooney

PUBLISHING INFORMATION:
Viking, 1979, HB, ISBN 0-670-53328-9
Penguin Puffin, 1983, PB, ISBN 0-14-050441-9

SUGGESTED AGES: 7–9

TOPICS: Families
Food
Seasons

THEME: Organization and hard work were necessary for farm families to provide a livelihood for themselves in times past.

Setting the Stage

How do you think people provided food and clothing for their families long ago before there were stores to supply everyone's needs? (If children have a sketchy background, the adult may need to explain briefly the basics of life on early American farms.)

Bridge

In today's story we will follow a New England farm family from long ago, as they lived and worked through the seasons to support themselves. Each month meant different kinds of work for each member of the family. As you look at the pictures and listen to the story, try to imagine what it would have been like to have been a boy or girl back then.

Discussion Questions

Logical Deductions:
What do you think the advantages would have been to a lifestyle like that of the family in the book? (Family unity, no stress.) . . . the disadvantages? (Hard work, boredom.)

Look at the picture of the man going to Portsmouth market and coming home. What has happened to the countryside? (The season has changed from autumn to winter.)

Why do you think the man chose that particular time of year to travel to the market? (Good weather, no pressing work at home, comfortable temperatures.) What would be wrong with winter? (Bad weather plus maple sugaring time.) . . . spring? (Wet weather plus crops to be planted and sheep sheared.) . . . summer? (Fields and crops need tending.) . . . early fall? (Harvesting.)

Personal Prophecy:
If you had been the girl or boy, how would you have felt all the time the father was gone? How would you have felt once your father returned home safely?

Significant Detail:
Look back over all the activities that the family did throughout the year. List as many different tasks as you can recall.

Personal Relevance:
Sometimes museums and schools demonstrate crafts from America's past. Have you ever watched any of these activities? If you could help with one, what would you choose?

Significant Detail:
How long did it take the man to get to Portsmouth Market? (Ten days walking.)

Logical Deduction:
If a man can walk an average of 10 miles per day, how far away from Portsmouth Market did the family live? (100 miles.)

Significant Detail:
What did the man buy at the shop in Portsmouth? (Iron kettle, embroidery needle, knife, and candles.)

Personal Prophecy:
If you had been the father and had been so short on money that you could only buy three of the four items, which would you have left out? How would you have explained your decision to the family?

Activities

Craft:
Weaving is an interesting handicraft for children to do. The teacher should do step 1 in Activity 48.

Writing:
Writing letters will help children to identify with each family member's feelings and concerns. The father's letter is last so that his letter can reflect his business activities before he leaves for home. See Activity 49.

The seasons set the work schedule for the family. Children can choose a season and compose a vertical poem, describing that particular season and its activities. Two other forms for seasonal poetry are haiku and five senses. The three types of poems are arranged as follows:

VERTICAL FORM

S . . . .
P . . . .
R . . . .
I . . . .
N . . . .
G . . . .

HAIKU

Title
5 syllables +
7 syllables +
<u>5 syllables</u>
17 syllables together that explain an aspect of the season

FIVE SENSES

Spring is pink and lavender
It tastes like . . .
It sounds like . . .
It smells like . . .
It looks like . . .
It makes me feel like . . .

Following are three examples of poetry for the seasons. The first is a vertical poem by Amy Van-Arsdale, age nine, of Englewood, Colorado:

White snow
Ice skating
Nice presents
Tinsel on Christmas trees
Entertaining sledding
Reindeer flying

The following is a haiku poem by Linda K. Garrity:

MOUNTAIN SPRINGTIME

Frozen mountain streams
Can relax their icy grip.
Spring will follow soon.

This five senses poem is also by Amy VanArsdale:

Fall is red and orange.
It tastes like pumpkin pie.
It sounds like leaves crunching.
It smells like turkey roasting.
It looks like geese flying.
It makes me feel like going trick or treating.

Cooking:
Children enjoy making homemade cornbread and butter, foods that were staples in early America.

CORNBREAD

1. Turn on oven to 350°.
2. Use a large bowl and wooden spoon to mix:
   1 cup flour
   1 cup cornmeal
   ¼ cup sugar
   4 teaspoons baking powder
   ½ teaspoon salt
3. Beat together 2 eggs and add to mix.
4. Add:
   ¼ cup oil
   1 cup milk
5. Grease a 4" × 8" loaf pan and pour in batter. (Or use a square baking pan and reduce baking time.)
6. Bake about 45 minutes or until lightly browned.
7. Slice and spread with butter and honey.

HOMEMADE BUTTER

1. Pour a 1 pint carton of whipping cream into a jar.
2. Screw the lid on tightly and shake until about half the liquid is turning solid and sticking to the side.
3. Drain the liquid away and place the butter in a plastic container and refrigerate.
4. After the butter has chilled, you can use the back of a spoon to press more liquid (buttermilk) out of your butter.
5. Have friends take turns with you. It takes about a half hour!

Name _____

Directions:

To create hand weaving, you will need:
    An 8″ × 11″ piece of heavy cardboard
    Yarn (fat yarn works best)
    Paper clip

1. Mark off ¼″ spaces across the two short sides of the cardboard. Make an even number on one side and an odd number on the other. Cut a small v-shaped notch at each mark.

2. Tape a long piece of yarn to one corner of the cardboard. Thread the yarn under each notch and back around the front as shown. Knot or tape each end.

3. Tie a piece of yarn to a paper clip. Using this as a needle, weave in and out across the width of the cardboard. Start 1″ from the top and stop 1″ from the bottom. Tie new pieces of yarn to the piece you are using when you run out or want to change color. Push all woven lines closely together.

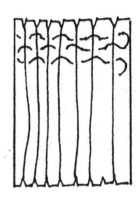

4. To remove the finished mat, cut the loops of yarn at the back of each notch. Tie the loose yarn ends together in a knot for fringe

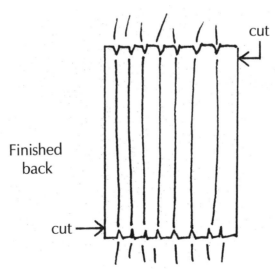

Finished back

cut

cut

Directions:

Members of the family would have thought often about the ox-cart man while he was gone. Pretend that you were each member of the family. Write a letter to your father or husband, telling him about happenings at home, the weather, and your feelings about his absence, and also asking questions about his trip. Then write a reply to the wife from the ox-cart man, telling about his trip. Try to imitate the four different styles of handwriting.

Dear Pa,	Dear Husband,
Love, Your daughter	Lovingly, Your Wife
Dear Pa,	Dear Wife,
Love, Your Son	Your Faithful Husband

The Pain and the Great One

AUTHOR: Judy Blume

ILLUSTRATOR: Irene Trivas

PUBLISHING INFORMATION:
Bradbury, 1984, LB, ISBN 0-02-711100-8
Dell, 1985, PB, ISBN 0-440-46819-1

SUGGESTED AGES: 6–9

TOPIC: Siblings

THEME: Children tend to feel that their siblings have the more favored roles.

Setting the Stage

Some of you have brothers or sisters. Others have cousins or friends that you play with. Raise your hand if you are one of the youngest in your family or play group. . . . one of the oldest. . . . or one of the middle children. Tell one good thing and one bad thing about your place in the group.

Bridge

Today we have a story called *The Pain and the Great One* by Judy Blume. It is about an older sister and a younger brother and the problems they have with their places in the family. Listen to see if some of their problems sound like yours!

Discussion Questions

Significant Detail:
Did the Great One have fun when she got to stay up later than the Pain? (No.) Why not? (She had no one to play with.) Did the Pain have fun when he got to play with all the building blocks by himself? (No.) Why not? (He had no one to play with.)

Logical Deduction:
Do you think the mother knew what would happen? (Yes.) What did she say to make you think that? (She said, "Remember that tomorrow.")

Personal Relevance:
Tell how you are most like the Pain or the Great One.

Personal Relevance:
The Great One can remember phone numbers and dial them correctly. What numbers are important for you to know?

Main Idea:
Whom do you think the parents liked best? Why? (They like both children the same, but that was difficult for the children to see.)

Personal Prophecy:
Pretend there is another chapter to this book, written by the mother and father. What are some things they could say about both children?

Personal Judgment:
Sometimes parents treat their different children differently. Decide when this is a good idea and when it is not a good idea.

Activities

Poetry:
A poem that The Pain could have written is "My Sister is a Sissy," by Jack Prelutsky, from *The New Kid on the Block*, page 138. See if you don't agree.

Drama:
Children can role-play their favorite scenes from the story, with some children taking supporting roles and one main character or narrator.

Craft:
Younger children often need extra telephone number practice. See Activity 50.

Writing:
Older youngsters can use the diary activity in two ways. They can either pretend that they are the characters from the story and write diary entries from their points-of-view or they can write entries about their own sibling(s). See Activity 51.

Directions:

Use this phone to practice your number. Color the phone.
Glue or tie a string to each hole.

My phone number is
_ _ _ - _ _ _ _

Directions:

Pretend you are the Great One. Tell about your brother in your diary.
Now pretend you are the Pain and tell about your sister.

Dear Diary,
My brother

Dear Diary,
My sister

The Patchwork Quilt

AUTHOR: Valerie Flournoy

ILLUSTRATOR: Jerry Pinkney

PUBLISHING INFORMATION:
Dial Books, 1985, HB, ISBN 0-8037-0097-0
Dial Books, 1985, LB, ISBN 0-8037-0098-9

SUGGESTED AGES: 6–9

TOPICS: Families
Grandmothers
Quilts

THEME: Handmade articles have a value beyond their cost.

Setting the Stage

Have you ever received a gift (not a toy) that you wanted to take special care of and save as a keepsake? What was it?

Bridge

Tanya, the little girl on the cover, and her grandmother worked a whole year to create an unforgettable keepsake. Let's listen to find out why that year and the keepsake will always stay in Tanya's heart.

Discussion Questions

Logical Deduction:
Why wasn't Mama very enthused about Grandma's quilt project at first? (She thought it would be a big mess.)

Personal Relevance:
Often craft projects are fairly messy. How does your mother or father react when you want to start a big project at home?

Logical Deductions:
Why do you think Mama changed her mind about the value of Grandma's and Tanya's quilt project? (She could probably see that it meant a lot to them.)

Grandma said that a quilt could "tell a story." How could it do that? (The fabric squares would remind the family of the occasions in which they wore the garments.)

Significant Detail:
Why did Grandma not tell the family of her illness during the Christmas celebration? (She didn't want to spoil anyone's fun.)

Personal Relevance:
Have you ever intentionally not told someone when you felt ill or had a pain because you didn't want to miss out on something special? What happened?

Personal Judgment:
For whom do you think the quilt project was more important—Tanya, who needed something to keep her hands and mind occupied during Grandma's long recovery; or Grandma, who needed something to give her the drive to recover?

Main Idea:
Why do you think the quilt will be special for Tanya, even though her mother could buy her a nice blanket? (The love that went into creating the quilt is far greater than its cost.)

Activity

Craft:
Children could create a quilt about themselves with each square representing one year in their lives. Uniform squares could be cut (pinking shears would add a "country" touch), and children could design each square plus decide on an overall pattern. Embroidery work on a fabric project would encompass many skills, though it would also involve much more time and expense.

See *The Quilt Story* for additional craft activities.

From *After the Story's Over: Your Enrichment Guide to 88 Read-Aloud Children's Classics*, published by Scott, Foresman and Company. Copyright © 1991 Linda K. Garrity.

Patrick's Dinosaurs

AUTHOR: Carol Carrick

ILLUSTRATOR: Donald Carrick

PUBLISHING INFORMATION:
Clarion, 1983, HB, ISBN 0-89919-189-4
Clarion, 1985, PB, ISBN 0-89919-402-8

SUGGESTED AGES: 5–7

TOPICS: Dinosaurs
Imagination

THEME: A child's imagination can play tricks on him or her.

Setting the Stage

Have you ever thought you saw something spooky or scary but you didn't want to tell anyone because you thought they might laugh? (The adult may want to relate a personal incident; this might be embarrassing to some children.)

Bridge

Something like that happened to Patrick after he spent a day at the zoo with his big brother Hank in this book. I wonder why this book by Carol Carrick is called *Patrick's Dinosaurs*? Let's listen to find out.

Discussion Question

Significant Detail:
Why does Hank know so much about dinosaurs? (He was older and went to school.)

Main Idea:
Tell why Hank does not see the same dinosaurs as Patrick. (They are not really there; Patrick is just imagining them.)

Significant Detail:
Where did Patrick feel safest? (In his own home.)

Personal Relevance:
Where do you feel safest?

Personal Prophecy:
Tell what you would do if you saw a dinosaur.

Personal Relevance:
Most children play "pretend" games like Patrick. What exciting "pretend" games do you like to play?

Personal Judgment:
Which brother, Patrick or Hank, is most like you? In what ways is he like you?

Activities

Poetry:
"One Day When We Went Walking," from *The Random House Book of Poetry for Children*, page 129, by Valine Hobbs, is a poem about a child who had a problem much like Patrick's. Try to decide what the problem was and how the child solved it.

Shel Silverstein has written a funny poem about a Brontosaurus—"If I Had a Brontosaurus," from *Where the Sidewalk Ends*, page 103. Listen carefully to see if you can figure out this poem.

Another funny dinosaur poem is, "I'd Never Dine on Dinosaurs" by Jack Prelutsky, from *The New Kid on the Block*, page 146.

Craft:
Dinosaurs are fun to make! Following are directions for clay dinosaurs as well as ones made from egg cartons. Younger children will need help attaching the head and tail on the egg carton version. See Activity 52.

Cooking:

DINOSAUR CLAY

1. Mix together in a large bowl with your hands:
   2 cups self-rising flour
   2 tablespoons alum
   2 tablespoons salt
2. Have an adult add 1¼ cups boiling water
3. Add:
   2 tablespoons oil
   a few drops of green food coloring
4. Mix with your hands until all ingredients are well-mixed.
5. You may divide clay into balls and make dinosaurs for a display.
6. Leave the dinosaurs out to get hard or put them away in a covered plastic container to use the clay again!

Directions:

To make a neat egg carton dinosaur, you will need a *cardboard* egg carton, 2 cardboard toilet paper rolls, 4″ × 4″ and 4″ × 2½″ green construction paper, white paper scraps for eyes and teeth, and green tempera paint.

1. Remove lid from egg carton and throw away.

2. Paint section with spiny dividers green.

3. Draw dinosaur head on 4″ × 4″ green construction paper. Cut out. Glue on teeth and eyes.

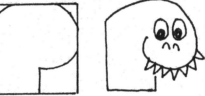

4. Bend a flap at the straight bottom of head. Glue head on end rim of carton.

5. Draw quarter-moon shaped tail. Cut out. Fold on end and glue to opposite end of egg carton.

FOLD

6. Cut 2 toilet paper rolls in half. Paint them green and let dry. Cut ½″ flaps along bottom. Tape or glue to bottom of carton.

7. Paint or color dots all over dinosaur.

From *After the Story's Over: Your Enrichment Guide to 88 Read-Aloud Children's Classics*, published by Scott, Foresman and Company. Copyright © 1991 Linda K. Garrity.

Peter's Chair

AUTHOR: Ezra Jack Keats

ILLUSTRATOR: Ezra Jack Keats

PUBLISHING INFORMATION:
Harper & Row, 1967, HB, ISBN 0-06-023111-4
Harper & Row, 1967, LB, ISBN 0-06-023112-2
Harper Trophy, 1983, PB, ISBN 0-06-443040-5

SUGGESTED AGES: 5–6

TOPICS: Chairs
Siblings

THEME: Young children often feel neglected when a new baby seems to dominate the household.

Setting the Stage

Have any of you had a new baby in the family? What changes did this create in your life?

Bridge

Peter, the little boy in today's story, has a new baby sister. I wonder what changes this creates for him and how he handles them? Let's find out in *Peter's Chair* by Ezra Jack Keats.

Discussion Questions

Significant Detail:
What did Peter dislike about having a new baby in the family? (He had to be quiet, and his parents were using his old furniture for the baby.)

Significant Detail:
How did Peter solve his problem with the new baby in the family? (He took his chair and ran away.)

Personal Prophecy:
How would you have solved the problem if you had been Peter?

Personal Judgment:
Do you think Peter would have felt the same way if the new baby had been a boy?

Logical Deduction:
Why do you think Peter wouldn't answer his mother when she asked him to come back? (Maybe he didn't want her to know right away that he was going to come back or maybe he wanted her to feel sad for neglecting him.)

Personal Judgment:
Think of some reasons why it might be a good idea to have baby furnishings and clothes in pink and blue. Think of some reasons why it might be a poor idea.

Main Idea:
Do you think Peter felt better about his new sister at the end of the story? (Yes.) Why do you think that? (He painted his old chair pink for the baby.)

Activities

Poetry:
Bobbi Katz's ''The Runaway,'' from *The Random House Book of Poetry for Children*, page 138, is a poem about a child who has feelings much like Peter's.

Craft:
The adult needs to precut the popsicle (or tongue depressor) sticks for the children to glue in Activity 53.

Directions:

Design your own chair, using popsicle sticks. Decorate with buttons, paint, marking pens, sequins, or anything you can think of to make the chair your very own. Print your name on the back.

A Pocket for Corduroy

AUTHOR: Don Freeman

ILLUSTRATOR: Don Freeman

PUBLISHING INFORMATION:
Viking, 1978, HB, ISBN 0-670-56172-X
Penguin Puffin, 1980, PB, ISBN 0-14-050352-8

SUGGESTED AGES: 5–6

TOPICS: Pockets
Teddy Bears

THEME: Pockets can help us keep track of our belongings.

Setting the Stage

Do you like having pockets on your clothing? What things do you like to put in your pockets? (The adult may want to add comments on the usefulness of pockets for himself/herself also.)

Bridge

Corduroy, Lisa's special bear, needed a pocket. How do you think he may have gotten a new pocket? Let's read *A Pocket for Corduroy* by Don Freeman to see if some of your ideas happened.

Discussion Questions

Significant Detail:
Why couldn't Lisa find Corduroy when it was time to leave the laundromat? (Corduroy crawled into a laundry bag, thinking it was a cave.)

Personal Relevance:
Corduroy likes to tell about things he's always wanted to do. Tell about some things you have always wanted to do or tell about some places you've always wanted to visit.

Getting lost can be very frightening for both parents and children. What should you do if you get lost?

Have you ever left something in your pocket that went through the wash? What happened to it? Let's see how many ways we can think of to help us remember to empty our pockets at night.

Personal Prophecy:
Think of all the ways that Corduroy could hold his belongings.

Personal Judgment:
Which story did you like best, *Corduroy* or *A Pocket for Corduroy*? Why did you like that one best?

Activities

Game:
Stitch up a deep pocket and fill it daily with a variety of objects. Have children close their eyes, reach into "Corduroy's Pocket," and try to identify one of the objects. This game can be played repeatedly because young children do not easily tire of it. It helps them to develop tactile perception, identification, and language skills.

Craft:
The simple craft that follows can also be used to create a bulletin board. See Activity 54.

Directions:

Children can make Corduroy from brown construction paper.
Cut out a pink or red heart for a pocket. Put a note for a friend inside.

The Polar Express

AUTHOR: Chris Van Allsburg

ILLUSTRATOR: Chris Van Allsburg

PUBLISHING INFORMATION:
Houghton Mifflin, 1985, HB, ISBN 0-395-38949-6

SUGGESTED AGES: 6–9

TOPIC: Christmas

THEME: Magic only comes to those who believe in it.

Setting the Stage

People believe *many* different things about Christmas. Lots of people do not celebrate Christmas at all. No one is right or wrong. If you do celebrate Christmas in your family, would you share one thing special that your family does?

Bridge

This cover makes me feel very curious about the story. Where do you think the train might be going? Who do you think might be riding on it? The story is about a boy's magical Christmas Eve adventure. Let's see what this train has to do with his adventure in *The Polar Express* by Chris Van Allsburg.

Discussion Questions

Significant Detail:
Why did the little boy lose the bell? (There was a hole in his pocket.)

Main Idea:
Why couldn't the mother and father hear the bell? (They didn't believe in Santa Claus.)

Personal Prophecy:
If you had been the little boy, what would you have asked Santa for?

Personal Judgment:
Most of the pictures in this book are dark and rather blurry. How did those pictures make you feel?

Logical Deduction:
Why does the bell still ring for the boy, even though he's now old?

Personal Judgment:
Do you think grown-ups should believe in Santa Claus? Why or why not?

Activities

Poetry:
"Dreams," by Langston Hughes, from *The Random House Book of Poetry for Children*, page 225, is a poem by a famous poet. It makes me think of our story. Listen and see if you can figure out why I think so.

Discussion/Writing:
Children could try to write an additional verse for the poem by making up a different metaphor.

Crafts:
The sound of the bell is an important feature in *The Polar Express*. Discuss the idea that certain sounds trigger different images and feelings within us. Have children close their eyes while you create different sounds using commonplace items such as an egg-timer, a whistle, plates clattering together. What pictures do these sounds bring to their minds? What are some of the pleasant and unpleasant sound-associations in their lives?

Children can make their own polar express.
Materials needed:
1. all sizes and shapes of boxes
2. construction paper
3. crayons
4. scissors
5. glue or paste

Each child can cut paper to create windows and wheels for his or her own car on the Polar Express. (See Figure 7).

Writing:

Writing an imaginary interview with Santa Claus would be fun. Questions about his home, age, and favorite foods would be good starters. A favorite quote, goals in life and accomplishments would also be interesting. Children could tape-record the interview, too.

Figure 7

The Quilt Story

AUTHOR: Tony Johnston

ILLUSTRATOR: Tomie de Paola

PUBLISHING INFORMATION:
Putnam, 1985, HB, ISBN 0-399-21009-1
Putnam, 1985, PB, ISBN 09-399-21008-3

SUGGESTED AGES: 7–9

TOPICS: Moving
Quilts

THEMES: Familiar objects, such as a homemade quilt, can help one cope with homesickness after a move.
For a young child, moving to a new place has always been unsettling.

Setting the Stage

There could be no better way to prepare children for a story about quilts than to show them an actual quilt! (Activity 55 can be used to provide background information before the story or as an extension after the story.)

Bridge

This quilt on the cover looks interesting. We don't often read stories about blankets! Do you think this is a modern girl on the cover? Why do you think that? Let's find out in *The Quilt* by Tony Johnston with pictures by Tomie de Paola.

Discussion Questions

Main Idea:
How did Abigail feel about moving? (It made her sad.) How did the quilt help? (It reminded her of home and brought her comfort.)

Significant Detail:
What happened to the old quilt in the attic? (A family of mice, a raccoon, and a cat lived in it and damaged it.)

Logical Deduction:
Do you think the little girl who discovered the quilt in the attic might have been a grandchild (descendent) of Abigail? (Yes.) What makes you think so? (The quilt was found in the same attic and there was a picture of Abigail in the girl's bedroom.)

Personal Relevance:
Have you ever used a blanket or stuffed animal to comfort you at night or when you were sick or sad? What is there about certain fabrics that seems to be so comforting?

Personal Judgment:
In your opinion, would moving to a new place be exciting (as you think of having a new home and making new friends) or sad (as you think of leaving your familiar home and old friends behind)?

Personal Prophecy:
Pretend you were Abigail, going west in a covered wagon. What do you think it would have been like?

Personal Judgments:
Would you have enjoyed being a pioneer child? Why do you feel that way?

Do you think moving far away would have been harder, easier, or about the same as today? Remember, there were no telephones then, though there was a very slow mail service and more time to write letters.

Personal Relevance:
What can you do to help a friend who has moved or is going to move? What can you do to help someone who has just moved into your neighborhood?

Activities

Research:
The background page can be duplicated and given to children for them to read or it can be read to them. See Activity 55.

Craft:
The obvious follow-up activity to *The Quilt Story* would be to make homemade quilts. It is only for the very ambitious! The first ditto sheet shows a quilt that can be created by using nine different pieces of fabric, stitched together, with an embroidered running stitch to outline sketches or words. Cutting the fabric for the second ditto sheet is more difficult. See Activity 56 and Activity 57.

Children could also create pieced quilts, using their own designs.

A simpler project can be achieved by using wallpaper or fabric samples for background pieces and plain-colored paper for appliques. Glue replaces needlework. (Use the shapes as patterns.)

Simpler yet, have children fill in the pages using markers or crayons.

Directions:

Read this article on quilts to yourself or follow along as your teacher reads it aloud. Then tell what you think is the most interesting fact that you learned about quilts.

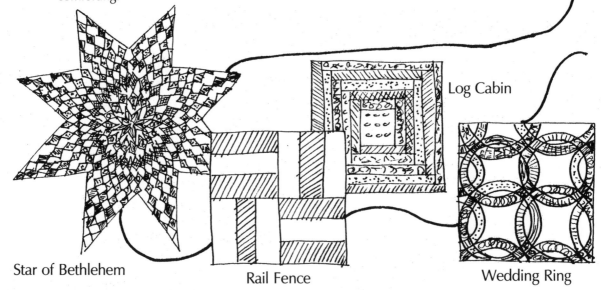

Quilts

Long ago, people's homes were not as warm and well-insulated as they are today. People needed many bedcovers to keep them warm during the cold months. They used leftover scraps of fabric sewn together to make a top layer for a quilt. Then they added other layers of cotton or feathers or even corn husks between the top and the plain bottom layer to make the quilt thick and warm.

Some women, being more artistic than others, designed beautiful tops for their quilts. Very old quilt tops were sewn together without a pattern or design. As fabric became more plentiful, pieces for quilt tops were cut into uniform squares or oblongs and sewn into patterns. These were called "pieced" quilts. Around 1750 the appliqué (ăp-plĭ-cāy′) quilt top became popular. It was made by cutting pieces of fabric into patterns and stitching them onto the quilt top with tiny stitches. The edges of the appliquéd pieces were turned under slightly as they were stitched to the quilt top. After women finished the pretty tops, they stitched the layers together by sewing around the patterns and designs on the top with tiny stitches both to add decoration and to prevent the stuffing from sliding all to one end inside the quilt. The quilts were fastened to large wooden frames to help the women sew on them.

Women often got together in homes or church basements to sew on quilts as they chatted with one another. Today quilting is an art form. Artists make quilts as decorative wall hangings, not to keep people warm at night. Electric blankets work better, but are not so lovely or comforting!

Log Cabin

Star of Bethlehem

Rail Fence

Wedding Ring

Directions:

Make a quilt about yourself. Draw pictures for each section and color them.

From *After the Story's Over: Your Enrichment Guide to 88 Read-Aloud Children's Classics*, published by Scott, Foresman and Company. Copyright © 1991 Linda K. Garrity.

Directions:

Make a quilt about yourself. Draw pictures for each section and color them.

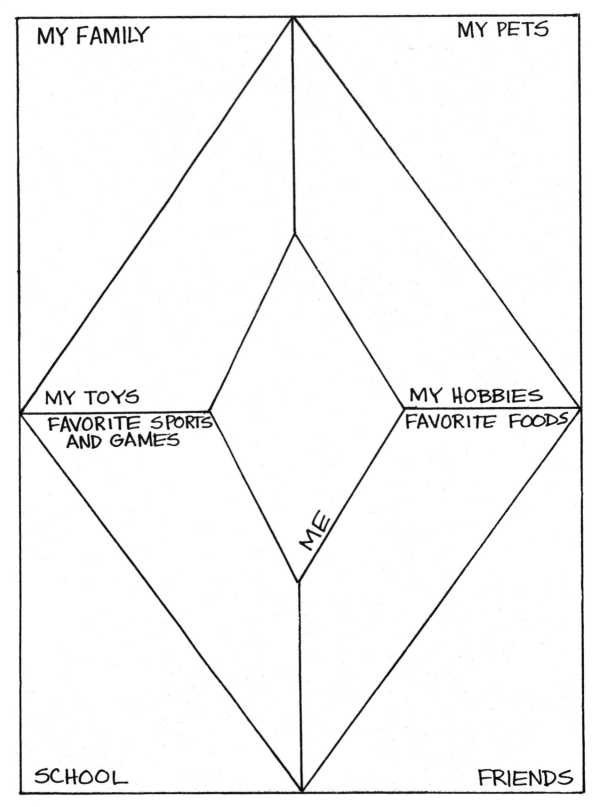

A Rabbit for Easter

AUTHOR: Carol Carrick

ILLUSTRATOR: Donald Carrick

PUBLISHING INFORMATION:
Greenwillow Books, 1979, HB,
ISBN 0-688-80195-1
Currently out of print.
Greenwillow Books, 1979, LB,
ISBN 0-688-84195-3

SUGGESTED AGES: 5–6

TOPICS: Easter
Pets
Rabbits

THEME: Learning responsibility can be difficult.

Setting the Stage

Do you have a pet you take care of? What do you have to do?

Bridge

Paul, the little boy on our cover, gets to take the kindergarten class's rabbit home for Easter vacation. Something terrible *almost* happens! Let's listen to *A Rabbit for Easter* to see what.

Discussion Questions

Significant Detail:
What did Paul need to do to take care of Sam? (Feed him raisins and pellets, give him water, and let him out to exercise.)

Logical Deduction:
What happened that scared Paul? (The rabbit got lost in the house.)

Personal Judgment
Pretend the rabbit was lost for good. Would it be easier for Paul if the rabbit had been his very own? Why do you feel that way?

Personal Relevance:
Stacey didn't want to share her new bicycle very much, did she? Have you ever played with other children who had a new toy they didn't want to share? How did you feel about that?

Significant Detail:
Where did they finally find Sam? (In the clothes basket.)

Main Idea:
Grown-ups call learning to remember and take care of things "being responsible." Do you think Paul learned to be responsible about caring for a pet? (Yes.)

Personal Relevance:
What is the most difficult responsibility that you have? (The adult could mention some examples.)

Activities

Crafts:
The stand-up Easter Egg decoration can be made with or without a boiled egg. See Activity 58.

The other activity is a simple identify and color page. See Activity 59.

Directions:

Color Sam as he is in the story.
Cut out around the dark line.
Cut slits on each end.
Cut around each bottom leg and foot. Bend forward.
Attach around egg. Glue on cottonball tail.

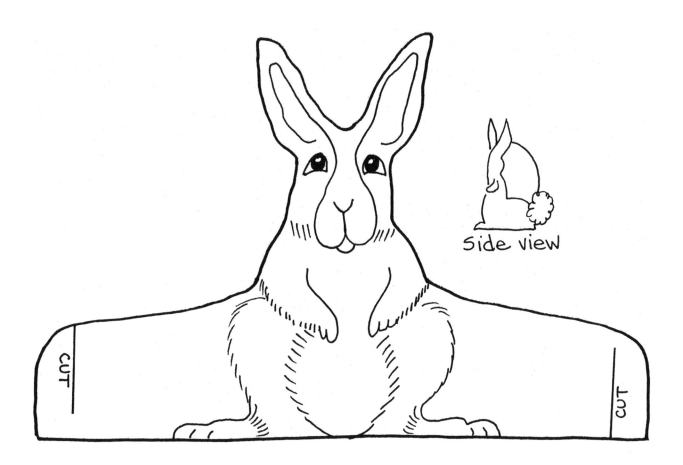

Side view

CUT

CUT

Directions:

Find the three rabbits that are exactly alike. Color them.

The Runaway Bunny

AUTHOR: Margaret Wise Brown

ILLUSTRATOR: Margaret Wise Brown

PUBLISHING INFORMATION:
Harper & Row, 1972, HB, ISBN 0-06-020765-5
Harper & Row, 1972, LB, ISBN 0-06-020766-3
Harper & Row, 1977, PB, ISBN 0-06-443018-9

SUGGESTED AGES: 5–6

TOPICS: Easter
Mother's Day
Rabbits

THEMES: Mothers don't want their little children to run away because they love them very much.
Sometimes it's easier too give up than to rebel.

Setting the Stage

Have you ever been mad at your mother about something? What caused you to forget about being mad?

Bridge

The little white bunny on the cover of our story is mad at his mother. He wants to run away from her. What do you think will happen? Let's listen to *The Runaway Bunny* by Margaret Wise Brown and see if you are right.

Discussion Questions

Significant Details:
Tell about some of the little bunny's ideas for getting away from his mother. (He thought of becoming a trout, a rock, a crocus, a bird, a sailboat, a trapeze artist, and a little boy.)

Tell about the ways his mother thought she could catch the little bunny. (She could become a fisherman, a mountain climber, a gardener, a tree, the wind, a tightrope walker, and a mother.)

Main Idea:
Why do you think the little bunny's mother was always able to think of a way to catch him? (Because she was bigger and wiser; because she loved him very much.)

Personal Prophecy:
Pretend you are the little bunny. Tell about a way to hide from the mother bunny. Now tell a way the mother bunny could find you.

Personal Relevance:
How would your mother feel if you ran away?

Significant Detail:
What did the little bunny do at the end of the story? (He decided to stay where he was and be her little bunny.)

Main Idea:
Why do you think the little bunny decided to quit trying to run away? (It was easier to give up rather than to rebel.)

Logical Deduction:
Why do you think it is a bad idea for little children to run away from their homes? (It upsets their parents; they could get hurt, and so on.)

Activity

Craft:
Activity 60 is a simple, stand-up craft for youngsters to make.

Directions:

Color this last scene from *The Runaway Bunny*.
Cut along the darkest black line around the bunnies.
Fold up on dotted line and you will have a standing picture.

Sometimes It's Turkey—Sometimes It's Feathers

AUTHOR: Lorna Balian

ILLUSTRATOR: Lorna Balian

PUBLISHING INFORMATION:
Abingdon, 1986, HB, ISBN 0-687-39074-5
Abingdon, 1990, PB, ISBN 0-687-37106-6

SUGGESTED AGES: 5–7

TOPIC: Thanksgiving

THEME: It is nearly impossible to kill a pet for food.

Setting the Stage

Have you ever enjoyed a nice Thanksgiving dinner? What is the most important part of the dinner?

Bridge

The title of this book is an odd one—*Sometimes It's Turkey—Sometimes It's Feathers* by Lorna Balian. I wouldn't want to eat feathers for my Thanksgiving dinner, would you? I wonder why the book is called that? Let's read and find out.

Discussion Questions

Main Ideas:
Do you think Mrs. Gumm and Cat will eat the turkey next Thanksgiving? (No, because they have grown too fond of him.)

Explain that the title, *Sometimes It's Turkey—Sometimes It's Feathers*, is the same as saying "It's either a feast or a famine," meaning there's either lots to eat or nothing. Why do you think the title is a good one? (They had planned on eating turkey for Thanksgiving, but would be eating something else instead.)

Logical Deductions:
Why do you think Mrs. Gumm was so excited about finding a turkey egg to raise for her Thanksgiving dinner? (She may have been too poor to buy a turkey or she might have just enjoyed raising animals.)

Show children the pictures of Mrs. Gumm's kitchen that show her wood range and hand water pump. You will need to offer some explanation of these kitchen appliances. Why does Mrs. Gumm use these things instead of sinks and faucets and stoves like those we have? (She may have been too poor or too old-fashioned, or the story may have happened a long time ago.)

Personal Judgment:
Many people do not like the idea of killing chickens, cows, and pigs to provide meat for people to eat. They eat other foods for a healthy diet. That means no fried chicken, hot dogs or hamburgers. How do you feel about this subject? Do you think it is all right or wrong to kill animals to feed people?

Significant Detail:
Turkey certainly ate a lot of different things, didn't he? What one food did he eat that seemed very unusual for a turkey? (Cat food.)

Logical Deduction:
How do you think that the cat felt about that? (The expressions on the cat's face show that he was growing fond of the turkey, so maybe he didn't mind.)

Significant Detail:
The pictures in this book are unusual. Why? (They are two-toned tan and white.)

Personal Judgment:
Do you like the choice of colors? What colors would you have used?

Activities

Poetry:
Shel Silverstein's "Point of View," from *Where the Sidewalk Ends*, page 98, is a poem with which Mrs. Gumm would agree. See if you can tell why after you have heard the poem.

Writing:
Pretend you are a neighbor of Mrs. Gumm and you know what happened to her at Thanksgiving. You want to invite her to a Christmas dinner at your home. You usually buy a turkey and trimmings for this meal. What should you serve this year? What are your reasons? Write a letter to Mrs. Gumm, inviting her to your dinner. Explain what you're going to serve and why.

Imagine that you are Mrs. Gumm's grandchild and she has invited you to spend the summer with her. What do you think you might do? Would you enjoy visiting her? Write a letter home to your parents, telling them about your summer with Grandma Gumm.

Craft:
This craft technique makes an outstanding turkey. See Activity 61.

From *After the Story's Over: Your Enrichment Guide to 88 Read-Aloud Children's Classics*, published by Scott, Foresman and Company. Copyright © 1991 Linda K. Garrity.

Directions:

Draw a large simple turkey on black construction paper.
Squeeze a heavy glue line from a bottle of white glue over all pencil lines.
Let dry overnight.
Color between the glue lines with bright oil pastels or colored chalk.

From *After the Story's Over: Your Enrichment Guide to 88 Read-Aloud Children's Classics*, published by Scott, Foresman and Company. Copyright © 1991 Linda K. Garrity.

Spectacles*

AUTHOR: Ellen Raskin

ILLUSTRATOR: Ellen Raskin

PUBLISHING INFORMATION:
Aladdin, 1972, PB, ISBN 0-689-70317-1
2nd edition, Aladdin, 1988, PB,
ISBN 0-689-71271-5

SUGGESTED AGES: 6–8

TOPIC: New Glasses

THEMES: Lack of correctional eyeglasses can cause a variety of problems.
Acquiring new glasses requires a certain amount of adjustment for children.

Setting the Stage

How many of you either wear glasses yourselves or have someone in your family who wears them? Would you tell about getting your glasses—who first thought you needed them, what was it like going to the eye doctor, and so on?

Bridge

Today we're going to hear some stories (a story) about children who needed to wear glasses (sometimes called *spectacles* or *specs*). Let's listen to how they reacted to their new glasses.

Discussion Questions

Significant Detail:
What did Iris do when her mom took her to the eye doctor? (Cried "No" to mother's suggestions.)

Main Ideas:
What problems did Iris have before she got her new glasses? (What she saw was distorted—she saw some very strange things.)

What happened after Iris got her new glasses? (She could see clearly, though she still removed her glasses at times to compare views.)

*See *Arthur's Eyes*, page 16 and *Watch Out, Ronald Morgan!*, page 207. (*Note:* All three stories deal with children getting new glasses. Any one of the three stories could be used alone, though the three blend together well to cover this topic.)

Star Mother's Youngest Child

AUTHOR: Louise Moeri

ILLUSTRATOR: Trina Schart Hyman

PUBLISHING INFORMATION:
Houghton Mifflin, 1975, HB, ISBN 0-395-21406-8
Houghton Mifflin, 1975, PB, ISBN 0-395-29929-2

SUGGESTED AGES: 7–9

TOPIC: Christmas

THEMES: Sometimes our dreams come true in unexpected ways.
Don't judge people by their appearances.
You can often change things if you will make the effort.

Setting the Stage

Have you ever wished for something and had your wish come true, but not in the way you had thought?

Bridge

This unusual story is about an old woman and a young star who both wished desperately for the same thing. Let's read *Star Mother's Youngest Child*, by Louise Moeri, to see how both their dreams came true in an unexpected way one Christmas.

Discussion Questions

Significant Detail:
What gift did the Old Woman give the Ugly Child? (A silver belt buckle.)

Logical Deduction:
Why did she hate to give it to him at first? (Because she had planned to wear it at her funeral; also, she didn't care for a boy who was so unattractive.)

Significant Detail:
What gift did the Ugly Child give the Old Woman? (The smells and sounds of Christmas.)

Personal Judgment:
Which gift was the best in your opinion? Explain why you feel that way.

Personal Prophecy:
If you had been the Old Woman, how would you have treated the Ugly Child?

Personal Judgment:
Do you think the Old Woman was wise to be leery of such an odd-looking child, or do you think she was wrong to judge him by his appearance?

Significant Detail:
What was the Old Woman's wish? (That she could celebrate Christmas.)

Logical Deduction:
Did her wish come true? (Yes.) How? (She made all the Christmas preparations to please the boy.)

Main Idea:
Could the Old Woman have made her wish come true without the Ugly Child? (Yes.) How? (She could have invited a guest and made the preparations.)

Activities

Poetry:
In "Merry . . .," from *Where the Sidewalk Ends*, page 164, Shel Silverstein has written a poem that begins with the same forlorn, somewhat self-pitying attitude with which our story begins. Like the story, the poem also has an unexpected twist at the end.

Writing:
Children can fill out this report card for the character from the story and then discuss it. See Activity 62.

This story lends itself to a dramatic interpretation. It works best with two strong main characters, simple props, and some costuming and face makeup. If taken seriously by youngsters, it can become a touching performance.

Directions:

Pretend that you are the teacher of Star Mother's Youngest Child. Fill in
the boxes on the report card with O's, S's, or N's. Then write your advice
to the child's mother on the bottom of the card.

Report Card for *Star Mother's Youngest Child*

O=Outstanding   S=Satisfactory   N= Needs Improvement

Beauty

Kindness

Intelligence

Obedience

Table Manners

Grace

Neatness

Curiosity

Additional Comments: _____

_____

_____

_____

The Sweet Touch

AUTHOR: Lorna Balian

ILLUSTRATOR: Lorna Balian

PUBLISHING INFORMATION:
Abingdon, 1976, HB, ISBN 0-687-40773-7
Abingdon, 1990, PB, ISBN 0-687-40774-5

SUGGESTED AGES: 5–7

TOPICS: Candy
Magic Wishes

THEMES: There can be too much of a good thing.
Greed can lead to problems.

Setting the Stage

What is your favorite sweet treat? (The adult should start this conversation, which should provoke lively interest.)

Bridge

Why do you suppose Peggy, the little girl on the cover of our story, has such a happy smile on her face? Yes, all those treats would make anyone smile. I wonder how she got all of that candy and if she is going to eat it all by herself? Let's listen to Lorna Balian's *The Sweet Touch* to find out.

Discussion Questions

Logical Deduction:
What do you think really happened? (Peggy had a dream.) What makes you think that? (On the last page we learn that Peggy awoke from some wild sleep because there are feathers all over and her quilt is twisted.)

Significant Detail:
Why did Peggy get only one magic wish? (Oliver the Magnificent Magic Genie was small and a new-comer in the magic business.)

Personal Prophecy:
If you had been Peggy, how could you have used your magic wish to avoid the problem Peggy got into?

Significant Detail:
What is unusual about the illustrations in this book? (They are black and white until the candy is intro-duced. The candy is in full color.)

Logical Deduction:
How did Oliver's mother undo the Magic Touch? (She helped him through the spell backwards.)

Activities

Poetry:
"Lester," by Shel Silverstein, from *Where the Side-walk Ends*, page 69, is a poem about a fellow with three magic wishes. He tried to be clever and use his wishes wisely, but he ended up outsmarting himself. Let's see what he did.

What if you had a magic touch that turned everything into raspberry gelatin? That was Shel Silverstein's idea when he wrote "The Squishy Touch," from *A Light in the Attic*, page 53.

Additional Reading:
The idea of magic wishes has always intrigued people. In fact, the Greek myth about King Midas and his Golden Touch is over 2,000 years old. Many folktales also use magic wishes and touches. *The Sweet Touch*, which younger children enjoy, and *The Chocolate Touch*, which is a novel for a little older child, are modern-day versions of these old tales. The following editions would be good additional read-alouds for contrast and comparison to *The Sweet Touch*.

Aladdin and the Wonderful Lamp, Andrew Lang, Viking, 1981.
The Chocolate Touch, Patrick Catling, Bantam, 1981.
The Fisherman and His Wife, Randall Jarrell, trans-lator, and Margot Zemach, illustrator, Farrar, 1980.
The Fisherman and His Wife, Elizabeth Shub, trans-lator, and Monika Laimgruber, illustrator, Green-willow, 1980.

King Midas and the Golden Touch, Nathaniel
Hawthorne, Harcourt, Brace, Jovanovich, 1987.
The Three Wishes, Paul Galdone, McGraw, 1961.
The Three Wishes, Margot Zemach, Farrar, 1986.

Craft:
Children enjoy the word scramble-coloring page.
See Activity 63.

Drama/Art:
Children could study newspaper and magazine ads
and then create ads for magic wishes or magic
touches. Some might enjoy presenting live
commercials.

Directions:

Unscramble the words in Peggy's machine to find her sweet wishes.
Color the picture.

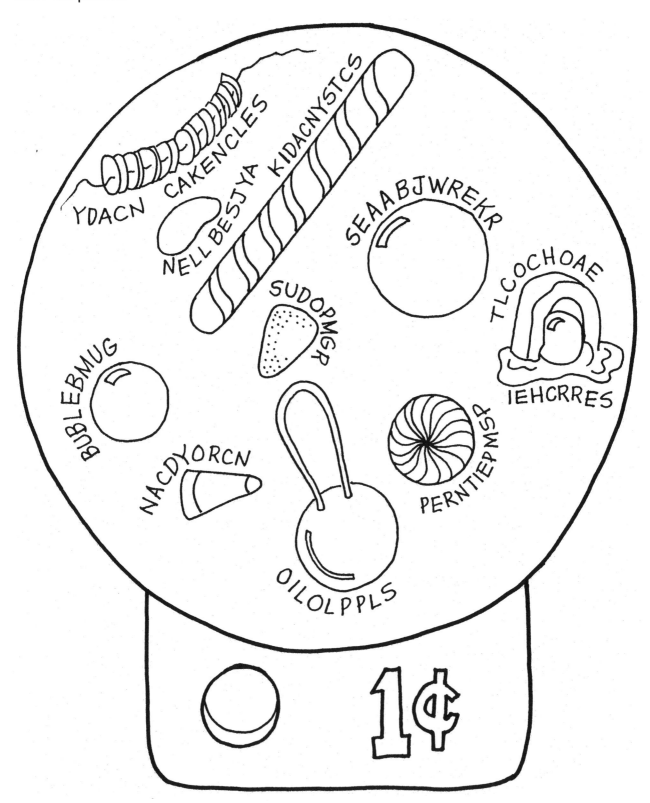

Sylvester and the Magic Pebble

AUTHOR: William Steig

ILLUSTRATOR: William Steig

PUBLISHING INFORMATION:
Windmill Books, 1969, PB, ISBN 0-671-96022-9
Simon & Schuster, 1988,
HB, ISBN 0-13-881707-3

SUGGESTED AGES: 5–7

TOPICS: Families
Magic Wishes

THEME: The most important thing in the world is to be with those who love you best.

Setting the Stage

If you had a magic pebble that would grant all sorts of magic wishes, what would you wish for?

Bridge

Sylvester, a little donkey in today's story, found a magic pebble. I wonder what Sylvester wished for? Let's listen to see how his magic wishes turned out in *Sylvester and the Magic Pebble* by William Steig.

Discussion Questions

Significant Detail:
Why did Sylvester make the decision to turn himself into a rock in the first place? (He was too frightened to think carefully.)

Personal Relevance:
Have you ever been so upset or frightened that you made a poor decision?

Significant Detail:
When Sylvester's mother and father were near the rock, Sylvester wanted to shout at them, but he couldn't. Why not? (He couldn't talk.)

Logical Deduction:
The book said that Sylvester was stone-dumb. What did that mean? (He was unable to talk, not that he wasn't smart.) (The pun used here probably was intended for adults only, though it creates a good opportunity to explain the meaning of "deaf and dumb" and "stone-deaf.")

Personal Relevance:
When parents and children are apart, they often realize how much they love one another. When you spend the day or night with someone else, do you ever wonder if your family is missing you? Toward the end of your stay away from home, do you start missing your family?

Main Idea:
Why didn't the Duncans start using their magic pebble to begin wishing for all sorts of new things? (They had their child back, which was all they really wanted.)

Activities

Drama:
This simple story lends itself well to creative drama. A few simple props such as a table, chairs, paper leaves and snowflakes, a picnic basket, and, of course, a red magic pebble are all you need.

Craft:
Children can make their own magic pebble. Hopefully, none will be operational. See Activity 64.

Writing:
The Missing Persons Report can be filled out, complete with a picture of Sylvester. See Activity 65.

Name _____ **Activity 64**

Directions:

Make your own magic pebble. Find a smooth interesting rock. Using acrylic paint or permanent markers, draw a picture or design on your rock. If you use permanent markers a coat of gloss medium or varnish will give a shiny finish. Keep your magic pebble in a secret place and use only for making important wishes.

Directions:

Fill out a Missing Persons Report for poor Sylvester. Draw a picture of Sylvester in the square.

Name _____

Age _____

Description _____

_____

_____

Last seen_____

_____

Those with information call: _____

The Tale of Peter Rabbit

AUTHOR: Beatrix Potter

ILLUSTRATOR: Beatrix Potter

PUBLISHING INFORMATION:
Various editions in PB, LB, and HB by different publishers.

SUGGESTED AGES: 5–6

TOPICS: Easter
Rabbits

THEMES: Natural consequences are usually punishment enough for disobedience. Children should heed their parents' warnings about danger.

Setting the Stage

All parents warn their children about dangers. From time to time, however, most children disobey and then discover why their parents had warned them about something. Have you ever disobeyed a direction, only to find out that your parents were right? (The adult should start the discussion by revealing a personal anecdote from childhood. NOTE: The anecdotes should reveal instances where the consequences of the disobedience led to an understanding of the parents' admonition, not punishment.)

Bridge

Notice how small our storybook is for today. The pictures are also very little, yet so interesting. The story and pictures were both done a long time ago by an English lady named Beatrix Potter. She first wrote the story as a letter to a little boy on September 4, 1893. Later the letter was made into a book called *The Tale of Peter Rabbit*.

Discussion Questions

Significant Details:
What did Flopsy, Mopsy, and Cottontail do while their mother was gone? (They went down the lane to gather blackberries.)

What did Peter do? (He went to Mr. McGregor's garden.)

Personal Prophecy:
If you had been a fifth little rabbit, would you have gone with Peter or with the other rabbits?

Logical Deduction:
Why do you suppose Peter went to the garden rather than to gather blackberries? (Maybe he preferred garden vegetables or maybe he was curious or craved excitement.)

Significant Detail:
What did his mother do when Peter came home without his jacket? (She wondered about it but did nothing.)

Main Idea:
Why do you think the mother did not punish Peter for losing his jacket and shoes? (Maybe she thought his illness was punishment enough.)

Personal Relevance:
What would your mother have done if you had come home without a new coat?

Personal Prophecy:
What do you think Peter will do the next time he goes out to play?

Main Idea:
Why do you think that? (He learned that his mother's warnings were correct.)

Personal Judgment:
Do you think the mother should have tried to find out what happened to Peter and punished him so he wouldn't do it again or just let it go, hoping he learned his lesson? Explain why you think your idea is better.

Activities

Cooking:

Camomile tea is sold in many grocery stores. A big pot would allow each child a sip, so he or she would know what it tastes like.

Craft:

Children can figure out the maze and then color the pictures. See Activity 66.

Directions:

Help Peter find his way out of Mr. McGregor's garden to the safety of the woods.

The Tenth Good Thing About Barney

AUTHOR: Judith Viorst

ILLUSTRATOR: Erik Blegvad

PUBLISHING INFORMATION:
Macmillan, 1971, HB, ISBN 0-689-20688-7
Aladdin, 1975, PB, ISBN 0-689-70416-X

SUGGESTED AGES: 5–9

TOPICS: Death
Pets

THEMES: Adjusting to the death of a beloved pet is difficult.
Views about an afterlife vary greatly.
Death is a part of the life cycle.

Setting the Stage

Have any of you ever had a pet die? When children have had a pet for a long time, it is very upsetting when the pet dies. Was the death of your pet a very sad time for you?

Bridge

Who do you think Barney is in the title? What do you think this family on the cover is doing? What clues make you think that? Let's see if our guesses are right in the book *The Tenth Good Thing About Barney* by Judith Viorst.

Discussion Questions

Main Idea:
Why do you think the mother suggested that they hold a funeral for Barney? (Because she thought it would help the boy adjust to his pet's death.)

Significant Detail:
What did Annie and the boy have a fight about? (Whether Barney was now in heaven or just in the ground.)

Personal Relevance:
Which child's viewpoint is closer to your own?

Personal Judgment:
Do you think it's interesting to compare views about death with others, or do you think it's wiser to avoid that subject? Explain why you feel that way.

Significant Detail:
What was the tenth good thing about Barney? (The cat's body would help grow flowers.)

Logical Deduction:
Why was that? (The body would decompose over a long period of time and enrich the soil.)

Activity

This story is usually read to children to help them cope with a pet's death. For that reason the book, coupled with the before-and-after discussion, is usually adequate to cover the topic without additional activities.

From *After the Story's Over: Your Enrichment Guide to 88 Read-Aloud Children's Classics*, published by Scott, Foresman and Company. Copyright © 1991 Linda K. Garrity.

Thanksgiving at the Tappletons'

AUTHOR: Eileen Spinelli

ILLUSTRATOR: Maryann Cocca-Leffler

PUBLISHING INFORMATION:
Harper & Row, 1984, HB, ISBN 0-201-15892-2
Harper & Row, 1989, PB, ISBN 0-06-443204-1

SUGGESTED AGES: 5–9

TOPIC: Thanksgiving

THEMES: Appreciating one's family and blessings is more the meaning of Thanksgiving than eating.
Avoiding unpleasantries does not help them disappear.

Setting the Stage

Who do you usually spend Thanksgiving with?

Bridge

Who do you think all these people might be on the cover of *Thanksgiving at the Tappletons'*? Let's see if we can find out who they all are and then see what happens at the Tappletons' in this book by Eileen Spinelli.

Discussion Questions

Personal Prophecy:
If you had been Mrs. Tappleton, what would you have done to prevent the disaster with the turkey?
... Mr. Tappleton   ... the pies?
... Kenny Tappleton   ... the salad?
... Jenny Tappleton   ... the mashed potatoes?

Main Idea:
Why did all the Tappletons try to hide their mistakes? (They were embarrassed and did not want to face the truth.) Did hiding the mistakes help in the end? (No.)

Personal Judgment:
When a person makes a mistake, should he or she: tell what happened right away, or wait a while and take a chance that others might forget about it or that things might improve anyway?

Personal Relevance:
Grandmother was the one who helped smooth over the disappointment with the missing food. There is usually one person in each family who tries especially hard to smooth over rough times. What person in your family usually does this? What does that person do?

Personal Prophecy:
What are some other ways the Tappletons could have solved their problem of having no meal to serve for Thanksgiving?

Logical Deduction:
Do you think the Tappletons would have realized the true meaning of Thanksgiving if they had not lost their turkey dinner? (Probably not.) Why do you feel that way? (They would have continued to take the meal for granted.)

Personal Judgment:
Why do you think it sometimes takes bad luck for people to appreciate what they have?

Activities

Poetry:
Grandmother's Thanksgiving poem was very touching and meaningful. A poem by Jack Prelutsky, "I'm Thankful," from *The New Kid on the Block*, pages 28–29, is written in a similar form. However, it's doubtful that you will find it touching, unless it touches your funnybone!

Grandmother's prayer is also a poem. "Thanksgiving," by Ivy O. Eastwick, from *The Random House Book of Poetry for Children*, page 47, is a poem that could serve as a prayer. Listen and decide which poem you prefer.

Writing:
What did Grandfather say each time another part of their meal was missing? (I'm hungry as (increasing number) of elephants.) Expressions using "as . . ." are called similes. What are some other similes expressing hunger? Children can recall or create

similes expressing hunger, writing and illustrating them on a sheet of white drawing paper.

Craft:

The Thanksgiving card can be used in several ways: children can create a poem or write a letter to the family or even copy a poetry selection on the inside of the card. Parents enjoy seeing their children's drawing and writing efforts. By adding the year, the project becomes something that many families like to save. See Activity 67.

Cooking:

The pumpkin pie recipe is delicious. The sandwich bag allows each child to neatly make an individual crust.

MINIATURE GRAHAM CRACKER CRUSTS

1. Place two graham crackers in a small plastic bag and crush thoroughly.
2. Pour crumbs into a foil muffin cup within a muffin tin.
3. Add:
   1 teaspoon sugar
   1 tablespoon melted butter
4. Stir together carefully.
5. Press the crust carefully around the sides and bottom of the muffin cup.
6. Pumpkin filling can be added now or the crusts can be baked for 8 minutes at 350°.

TAPPLETONS' PUMPKIN MINI-PIES

1. In a large pan add:
   2 cans pumpkin (16 oz.)
   2 1-pound bags of large marshmallows
   2 teaspoons cinnamon
   ½ teaspoon salt
   ½ teaspoon cloves
   ½ teaspoon ginger
   ½ teaspoon nutmeg
   2 teaspoons vanilla
2. Cook over low heat, stirring until marshmallows are melted.
3. Cool to room temperature.
4. Gently fold 2 cartons of whipped topping (about 4 cups) into mixture.
5. Spoon into individual pies. (Makes 24–30 cupcake-sized pies.)
6. Freeze overnight.
7. Thaw shortly before eating.

From *After the Story's Over: Your Enrichment Guide to 88 Read-Aloud Children's Classics*, published by Scott, Foresman and Company. Copyright © 1991 Linda K. Garrity.

Directions:

Make a Thanksgiving card for your family. Fold 9″ × 12″ construction paper in half. Draw a picture of your family and guests at Thanksgiving dinner on 8″ × 11″ white construction paper. Color. Glue to front of card. Write a letter, poem or message inside.

Our Family

Thanksgiving (Year)
I am thankful for my family.
I am thankful for my home.
I am thankful for my friends.
I am thankful for good food.
I am thankful for warmth
                    and love.
Most of all,
        I am thankful for YOU.

From *After the Story's Over: Your Enrichment Guide to 88 Read-Aloud Children's Classics*, published by Scott, Foresman and Company. Copyright © 1991 Linda K. Garrity.

That Terrible Halloween Night

AUTHOR: James Stevenson

ILLUSTRATOR: James Stevenson

PUBLISHING INFORMATION:
Greenwillow, 1980, HB, ISBN 0-688-80281-8
Greenwillow, 1980, LB, ISBN 0-688-84281-X

SUGGESTED AGES: 6–8

TOPICS: Grandfathers
Halloween
Imagination
Monsters

THEME: Children aren't the only ones who enjoy playing Halloween pranks.

Setting the Stage

Have you ever been in a Halloween haunted house at a party? What was it like?

Bridge

What is this creature on the cover of our story? Let's see what it is and what it does to poor Grandpa in *That Terrible Halloween Night* by James Stevenson.

Discussion Questions

Significant Detail:
When Louie and Mary Ann asked Grandpa what day it was, what did he say? (It was October 31, according to the paper.)

Logical Deduction:
Do you think Grandpa actually did not know that it was Halloween? (No, he knew but he wanted to fool the children.)

Why wasn't Grandpa scared by Louie and Mary Ann's tricks? (He could see through them.)

Personal Judgment:
What do you think was the scariest part of Grandpa's Halloween night?

Logical Deduction:
Do you think that that adventure really happened to Grandpa? (No.) Why do you think that? (Monsters are imaginary, and you can't turn into an old man overnight.)

Main Idea:
Why do you think Grandpa told that story to the children? (He enjoyed playing a prank on them.)

Personal Relevance:
Have you ever told someone, especially someone younger, a big story just to see their reaction? What did you tell them?

Personal Judgment:
When would it be wrong to tell a big story, and when would it just be fun for everyone?

Activities

Poetry:
"Its Fangs Were Red," by Jack Prelutsky, from *The New Kid on the Block*, page 22, is a poem that Grandpa would love. The drawings for *The New Kid on the Block* were done by James Stevenson, who also illustrated *That Terrible Halloween Night*.

Writing:
Have children write to their grandparents or another older relative or friend, asking about their scariest or funniest Halloween from their childhood.

Write or draw what happened behind the purple striped door.

Craft:
Talk about protective features that a variety of animals have, for instance, camouflage coloring, fangs, hooves, speed, odor. Then have children design and write about a super animal that would be "the best parts of a lot of things."

Children can use old magazines, especially those that have nature and animal features, to cut out various animal body pieces to create an animal monster; or they can use the duplicating page for a similar activity. See Activity 68.

From *After the Story's Over: Your Enrichment Guide to 88 Read-Aloud Children's Classics*, published by Scott, Foresman and Company. Copyright © 1991 Linda K. Garrity.

Directions:

Make your own monster from "the worst parts of a lot of things." Draw a body on another piece of paper. Color and cut out the body parts on this page. Glue some or all of the things on your body drawing any way you like. Add your own ideas.

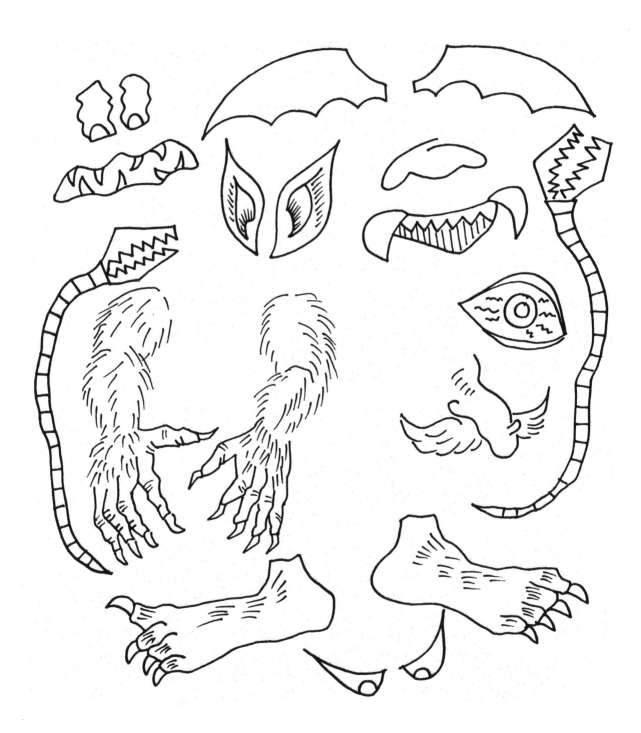

There's a Nightmare in My Closet

AUTHOR: Mercer Mayer

ILLUSTRATOR: Mercer Mayer

PUBLISHING INFORMATION:
Dial, 1968, HB, ISBN 0-8037-8682-4
Dial, 1968, LB, ISBN 0-8037-8683-2
Dial, 1976, PB, ISBN 0-8037-8574-7

SUGGESTED AGES: 5–6

TOPICS: Fear of Dark
Monsters

THEMES: Most children are uncomfortable with sights and sounds in the dark.
It is better to do something constructive about a nighttime fear than lie there in fear.

Setting the Stage

When I was little, I used to be afraid when I went to bed that . . . (Nearly everyone has had some childhood fear of the dark. If the adult begins with an anecdote of this nature, the children will more readily chime in with tales of their fears.) What is scary in your room when you go to bed?

Bridge

Look at the picture on the cover of today's story. How do you think the little boy feels? What do you think is frightening him? Let's read *There's a Nightmare in My Closet* to find out if you are right about this boy and what he does about it.

Discussion Questions

Significant Detail:
What did the little boy do every night before he went to bed? (He closed his closet door.) Why did he do that? (He didn't want the monster in the closet to get him.)

Logical Deduction:
Why did he decide to do something different to solve his monster problem? (He wanted to get rid of the nightmare once and for all, or maybe he was tired of being afraid.)

Main Ideas:
What happened when the little boy decided to go after the monster? (The monster cried and the boy had to comfort him.)

Mercer Mayer wrote this story for boys and girls your age. What do you think the story was telling you? (There really aren't monsters.)

Personal Prophecy:
If you had been the little boy, what other ways would you have tried to solve the monster problem?

Personal Judgments:
Why do you think most children and many adults dislike the darkness?

Do you think it is a better idea to just tell yourself that there are no monsters in the dark and go on to sleep, or to turn on the lights and see for yourself that there's not a monster there? Explain why you think so.

Activities

Poetry:
Here is a funny poem—"Afraid of the Dark," by Shel Silverstein, from *Where the Sidewalk Ends*, page 159—about a boy who is afraid of the dark. It has a very silly ending!

Where do bats live? Are caves dark or well-lit? Let's see why you would need to know that to see the humor in the poem "Batty," by Shel Silverstein, from *A Light in the Attic*, page 139.

This poem—"What's That?" by Florence Parry Heide, from *The Random House Book of Poetry for Children*, page 201—is meant to be scary! Let's listen and see if it scares you!

Writing:
Children could draw pictures or write about the scary sights and sounds in their rooms in the night.

Craft:
The craft activity requires an extra sheet of paper in addition to the duplicating page. Younger children will need a little assistance getting started on cutting out the door. See Activity 69.

Directions:

Color the picture. Cut around the door on the *darkest line only*. Glue the picture onto a plain white sheet that is the same size. Do not glue the door. Open the door and draw your own nightmare in the closet.

There's No Such Thing as a Chanukah Bush, Sandy Goldstein

AUTHOR: Susan Sussman

ILLUSTRATOR: Charles Robinson

PUBLISHING INFORMATION:
Whitman, 1983, LB, ISBN 0-8075-7862-2

SUGGESTED AGES: 8–9

TOPICS: Chanukah
Christmas

THEMES: Because of all the hoopla and gifts surrounding Christmas, it is a difficult time of year for Jewish children.
One can share the joy of others' religious celebrations without losing one's own religious identity.

Setting the Stage

Can anyone explain the meaning of Chanukah (hän'-ə-kə)? And the meaning of Christmas? (The adult will probably need to answer these questions, which are crucial to the understanding of the story.)

Bridge

Look at the cover of our story, *There's No Such Thing as a Chanukah Bush, Sandy Goldstein*. What two holiday symbols do you see? I wonder how these two symbols figure in our story. Let's listen and find out.

This book can easily be read in two sittings; divide at the end of Chapter 4.

Discussion Questions to Follow Chapters 1–4

Significant Detail:
Why wouldn't Robin's mother allow her to have a Christmas tree? (Because Jews do not observe Christmas.)

Logical Deduction:
Why wouldn't her mother allow her to have a Chanukah bush? (Her mother felt it was really just a Christmas tree by a different name.)

Personal Relevance:
Robin's mother explained that Jews found different ways to be Jewish. Are there also different ways to be Christian? (Yes.) Tell about as many different Christian religions, customs, or beliefs as you know.

Main Idea:
Why did Robin cry herself to sleep? (She felt badly about not being allowed to celebrate Christmas.)

Personal Judgment:
Do you think it was unfair of Robin's parents to be strict about not allowing Robin to observe Christmas, yet at the same time being tolerant of Grandpa planning a Christmas party for his union? Or do you think that the grown-ups knew what they were doing and shouldn't have had to explain themselves to Robin?

Bridge

What do you think is going to happen at the party? We'll find out if your guesses are right when we finish the story.

Discussion Questions to Follow Chapters 5–9

Significant Detail:
What did Robin do when her grandpa introduced her to his friends? (She looked down at the floor and wouldn't speak.)

Personal Relevance:
When your parents introduce you to grown-ups, what do you do? How do you feel?

Personal Judgment:
What do you think children should do when they are introduced to adults?

Personal Relevance:
Robin was very anxious about her first experience with Santa. Can you remember a first experience when you visited Santa? Was it scary? Why do you think most young children have mixed feelings about a chat on Santa's knee?

Logical Deduction:
Robin was quite surprised that Julie did not have a tree. What would be some reasons why people other than Jews would not have Christmas trees every year? (Lack of money, not enough space, no interest, belonging to non-Christian and other Christian religious and ethnic groups.)

Main Idea:
What did Robin do to share her special heritage? (She invited her Christian friend to enjoy the last evening of Chanukah with her family.)

Activities

Poetry:
Robin could have shared this poem by Aileen Fisher with her Christian friends as a part of her family's Chanukah celebration: "Light the Festive Candles," from *The Random House Book of Poetry for Children*, page 48.

Writing:
Information for the creative writing activity can be drawn from the book or from real-life experiences. See Activity 70.

Craft/Game:
Many dreidl patterns are fun for children to make, but they soon fall apart when handled. This dreidl will hold up better than most during play. See Activity 71.

Directions:

Pretend that you are hosting both a Christmas and a Chanukah party for your friends. Think about the refreshments and entertainment that would be appropriate for each celebration. Then create an imaginary invitation for your party.

You're Invited
to
a Chanukah Celebration

Where: _____
Date: _____ Time: _____
Please bring: _____
Please wear: _____
Refreshments served: _____
Activities: _____
R.S.V.P. by: _____

You're Invited
to
A Christmas Eve Party

Where: _____
Date: _____ Time: _____
Please bring: _____
Please wear: _____
Refreshments served: _____
Activities: _____
R.S.V.P. by: _____

Directions:

To make a star of David ornament, glue together colored cocktail toothpicks to form two equilateral triangles. Let dry. Invert one triangle and glue it over the other to make the star. Tie yarn at top to hang.

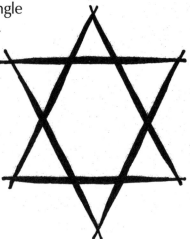

A simple dreidl is easy to make from the spine section of an egg carton. Draw symbols on sides with a marker. Push a short pencil through the section. Children spin the dreidl and do what the letters say.

נ Nun = You take nothing from pot.

ג Gimel = You take all.

ה Hay = You take half.

ש Shin = You put in half.

The four letters stand for *Nes Gadol Haya Sham* ("A great miracle happened here").

Through Grandpa's Eyes

AUTHOR: Patricia MacLachlan

ILLUSTRATOR: Deborah Kogan Ray

PUBLISHING INFORMATION:
Harper & Row, 1980, LB, ISBN 0-06-024043-1
Harper Trophy, 1983, PB, ISBN 0-06-443041-3

SUGGESTED AGES: 6–9

TOPICS: Grandfathers
   Handicaps—Blindness

THEME: Blindness requires special accommodations, though it does not limit enjoyment of the richness of life.

Setting the Stage

What do you think it would be like to be blind? (The adult needs to survey and fill in children's background knowledge on Braille, seeing-eye dogs, and other aspects of coping with blindness. Having children close their eyes and do a simple task can easily raise awareness.)

Bridge

The grandfather on the cover of our book is blind. He often takes care of his grandson. What problems do you think the grandfather might run into? Let's read *Through Grandpa's Eyes* by Patricia MacLachlan and see if your concerns are a problem for Grandpa.

Discussion Questions

Logical Deduction:

Why do you think John enjoys staying with his Grandpa so much? (He is fascinated with his Grandpa's ways of coping with blindness, and he enjoys the love and warmth of the older couple.)

How can Grandpa tell what is cooking and what is happening in the house? (He uses his ears and nose to hear and smell.)

Personal Relevance:

Grandpa says that he can hear Nana's voice smiling to him. Often grown-ups will say something that actually could be cross, but their tone of voice says that they are just kidding. When has this happened to you with a grown-up?

Personal Judgment:

Do you think that, because of his blindness, Grandpa enjoys such things as music, the out-of-doors (nature), art, and good food more or less than a person who can see?

Significant Detail:

Grandpa is able to do *almost* anything. What one thing did he not do? (He didn't realize that the light was on instead of off.)

Logical Deduction:

Do you think that he would have made that mistake if the light had had a wall switch instead of a chain? (No, you can feel if the switch is up or down. Of course, a two-way switch could still fool him.)

Personal Prophecy:

If you had been John, would you have told Grandpa right away that the light was still on or would you have waited until Grandpa was gone and then fixed it yourself? Why would you have chosen that way of handling it?

Activity

Craft:

This activity will give children an opportunity to work with Grandpa and Nana's system of food organization. Younger children may need to write in the clock numbers to do the project. After the cut-and-paste is finished, call off the different foods with their time designations, having the children close their eyes and find them on their plates, using Grandpa's method. See Activity 72.

Directions:

Cut out and glue the following: Grandpa's eggs at 9 o'clock; his toast at 2 o'clock; and his spoonful of jam at 6 o'clock. Add his bacon at 12 o'clock and his banana at 4 o'clock.

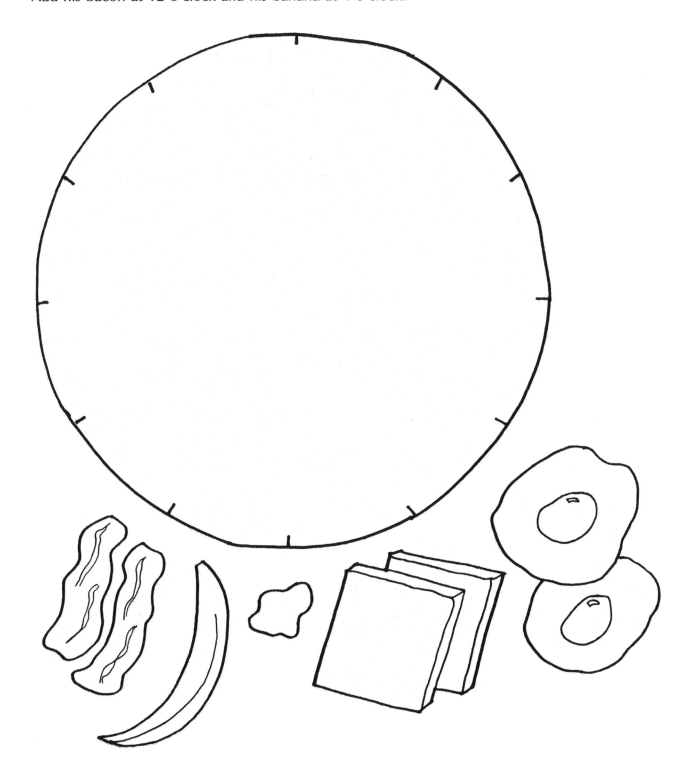

Tight Times

AUTHOR: Barbara Shook Hazen

ILLUSTRATOR: Trina Schart Hyman

PUBLISHING INFORMATION:
Viking, 1979, HB, ISBN 0-670-71287-6
Penguin Puffin, 1983, PB, ISBN 0-14-050442-7

SUGGESTED AGES: 6–8

TOPICS: Families
Pets

THEME: A family's love for one another can help them through a crisis.

Setting the Stage

What do you think "tight times" in a family would mean? (If the term is unfamiliar, explain that it refers to a shortage of money for the family.) In all families, the children occasionally ask for things that the family can't afford. What do your parents say when they think you are asking for something unreasonable?

Bridge

The little child on the cover of today's story doesn't look very happy. What is on the fork? (A lima bean.) Do you think the unhappiness is caused by the lima beans or the "tight times" mentioned in the title? Let's read this story by Barbara Shook Hazen and find out.

Discussion Questions

Significant Detail:
Why wouldn't the parents let the child have a dog? (They couldn't afford one.)

Personal Relevance:
Have you ever asked for a particular pet and your parent said you couldn't have it? What reasons did he or she give for not letting you have a pet? Did you accept that or did you continue to ask for the pet?

Logical Deductions:
How would the loss of the father's job affect "tight times" in the family? (It would make it worse.) Why would that be? (They would have even less money with his salary gone.)

Did the mother and father cry because the milk made such a mess on the floor? (No.) Why did they cry? (Their problems seemed too much for them to handle.)

Do you think the cat named Dog is going to eat the lima beans? (No.) Why not? (Cats don't eat vegetables.)

Personal Judgment:
The little child had never seen the father cry before. That is true in many families. Yet fathers must feel sad like everyone else. Why do you think so many of them never let their children see them cry?

Main Idea:
Do you think this family is going to make it through their "tight times"? (Yes.) What makes you think that? (The father is looking in the paper for work; the parents look as if they may have some plans; they know they have each other.) *Note:* It would seem natural to ask children a personal relevance question about difficult times in their own families. However, because of the sensitive nature of the subject, the adult may choose not to ask that question and hope that youngsters would gain some comfort from hearing this story about another family's surviving its difficulties.

Activity

Interviews:
Talk to older people about the Great Depression. There are many books and films that highlight this period of history. Then have the class brainstorm questions for interviews with people who lived through the Depression. Children could then write to or personally interview older people (they would have to be at least sixty years old) about their experiences in living through national "tight times."

From *After the Story's Over: Your Enrichment Guide to 88 Read-Aloud Children's Classics*, published by Scott, Foresman and Company. Copyright © 1991 Linda K. Garrity.

The Trouble with Mom

AUTHOR: Babette Cole

ILLUSTRATOR: Babette Cole

PUBLISHING INFORMATION:
Putnam, 1986, PB, ISBN 0-698-20624-X

SUGGESTED AGES: 5–8

TOPICS: Halloween
Mother's Day

THEME: Appearances are deceiving.

Setting the Stage

Have you ever felt embarrassed by something someone in your family did or said?

Bridge

The little boy in the center of the cover has a reason to feel embarrassed about his mother. Let's see if we can discover what it is and what the mother does about it in *The Trouble with Mom* by Babette Cole.

Discussion Questions

Significant Detail:
Why didn't Mom seem to get along with the other parents? (She turned them into toads and made freaky cupcakes.)

Personal Prophecy:
How would your mother have felt about the mother in the story? Would she have allowed you to go play at the boy's home?

Logical Deductions:
Why do you think the children reacted so differently from the adults about Mom? (They saw the weird things as fun. Children tend to be more accepting of unusual things than adults.)

How do you think the boy felt when the other parents told Mom off? (Embarrassed, upset, and maybe sad or angry.) Look at the next to last page. How did the boy feel now? (Proud and happy.)

Personal Judgment:
What do you think the boy should have done—tried to change his mother to fit in with others, tried to get others to understand her better, or just ignored the other people? Why do you think your idea would be the best?

Significant Detail:
What happened to change the other parents' opinion of Mom? (Mom put out the school fire and saved all the children's lives.)

Main Idea:
What do you think the other parents learned from this situation? (Not to judge people by appearances.)

Personal Prophecy:
How do you think they will act if an unusual family comes to their school in the future?

Activities

Writing:
The report card activity reflects the before-and-after aspect of the story. See Activity 73.

Older children can use their creativity in the "Letters to the Editor" activity. As an aid, they might look at the editorial page of a newspaper prior to beginning the project. See Activity 74.

Directions:

Fill in a report card for Mom by using *O*'s, *S*'s, and *N*'S. The first grading period refers to Mom at the beginning of the story. The second grading period refers to Mom at the end of the story. Write your opinion of Mom's behavior under the section on additional comments.

A Report Card for _____ Mom

1st Grading Period

O = Outstanding
S = Satisfactory
N = Needs Improvement

Appearance
Cooking Skills
Magic Skills
Creativity
Gets along well with children
Gets along well with parents

Additional Comments:

2ND Grading Period

Appearance
Cooking Skills
Magic Skills
Creativity
Gets along well with children
Gets along well with parents

Additional Comments:

Directions:

Pretend you are the four different people writing letters to the editor about the actions of Mom in the book *The Trouble with Mom*. Try to imitate the same style of handwriting used in each letter.

Letters to the Editor

Dear Editor,

_____

_____

_____

_____

_____

_____

_____

_____

_____

Signed,
an angry Parent

Dear Editor,

_____

_____

_____

_____

_____

_____

_____

_____

_____

Signed,
a Supportive Parent

Dear Editor,

_____

_____

_____

_____

_____

_____

_____

_____

_____

Signed,
The Neighborhood Kids

Dear Editor,

_____

_____

_____

_____

_____

_____

_____

_____

_____

Signed,
Equal Rights for
Supernaturals Society

The Velveteen Rabbit

AUTHOR: Margery Williams

ILLUSTRATOR: Various

PUBLISHING INFORMATION:
Various editions in PB, LB, and HB by different publishers

SUGGESTED AGES: 5–8

TOPICS: Rabbits
Toys

THEME: Belief in a toy can make it seem very real to a child.

Setting the Stage

What is it about stuffed animals that makes you want to touch them and play with them and take them to bed with you?

Bridge

The little boy in our story must have felt the same way you do because he slept with the soft, stuffed rabbit that you see on the cover. Then one day something strange and wonderful happened to his rabbit. What do you think that might have been? Let's listen to *The Velveteen Rabbit*, by Margery Williams, and find out.

Discussion Questions

Significant Detail:
Who was the only animal in the nursery that was kind to the Velveteen Rabbit? (The skin horse.)

Personal Relevance:
Have you known children who acted like the expensive toys in the nursery, thinking they were better than others for some reason or another?

Have you ever had a doll or stuffed animal that seemed real to you? (The adult may want to begin this discussion with a personal remembrance.)

Logical Deductions:
How did the Velveteen Rabbit become real to the boy? (The boy had spent so much time with the toy that it seemed real to him, or the nursery magic did it.)

Do you think the little boy was rich or poor? (Rich.) What makes you think that? (His clothes, his home, and the nanny to care for him.)

Significant Detail:
Why did the doctor want the Velveteen Rabbit destroyed? (He thought it would spread the scarlet fever germs.)

Logical Deduction:
Do most people destroy their children's toys after they have been sick to get rid of germs? (No.) Why not? (Germs die after a short time when they are not on a body.)

Significant Detail:
How did the Velveteen Rabbit become a real rabbit? (The fairy turned him into one.)

Personal Prophecy:
Do you like the ending? If you could change it any way you want, how would you have the story end? Remember, you may want to use magic, since it is used in the story already.

Activities

Poetry:
The Velveteen Rabbit is a famous, old story that thousands and thousands of children have heard over the years. "The Duel," from *The Random House Book of Poetry for Children*, page 174, is an equally old and famous poem by one of America's beloved children's poets, Eugene Field. It too is about the secret life of stuffed animals.

Craft:
The craft activity can be done either with pastel colored paper (appoint a few "ear experts" to help others cut around the ears) for a simple project, or it can be done with lovely ribbon and velveteen for a rather elegant bookmark gift for youngsters. See Activity 75.

From *After the Story's Over: Your Enrichment Guide to 88 Read-Aloud Children's Classics*, published by Scott, Foresman and Company. Copyright © 1991 Linda K. Garrity.

Directions:

To make a Velveteen Rabbit bookmark you will need
    1 yd. (or less) velveteen cloth (for an entire class);
    1 yd. of 2″ ribbon for every 6 bookmarks;
    tiny buttons or beads (optional).
Cut out rabbit and use as a pattern for rabbit cut out of velveteen.
Glue onto top of ribbon.
Decorate with button or bead eyes and nose if desired.

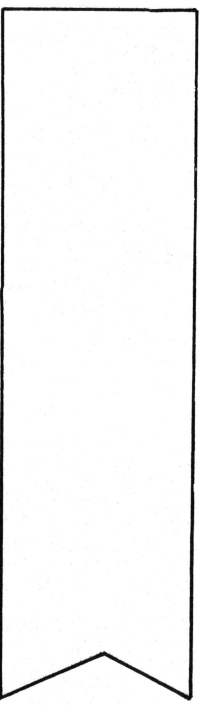

Watch Out, Ronald Morgan!*

AUTHOR: Patricia Reilly Giff

ILLUSTRATOR: Susanna Natti

PUBLISHING INFORMATION:
Viking, 1985, HB, ISBN 0-670-80433-9
Penguin Puffin, 1986, PB, ISBN 0-14-050638-1

SUGGESTED AGES: 6–8

TOPIC: New Glasses

THEMES: Lack of correctional eye glasses can cause a variety of problems.
Acquiring new glasses requires a certain amount of adjustment for children.

Setting the Stage

How many of you either wear glasses yourselves or have someone in your family who wears them? Would you tell about getting your glasses—who first thought you needed them, what was it like going to the eye doctor, and so on?

Bridge

Today we're going to hear some stories (a story) about children who needed to wear glasses (sometimes called *spectacles* or *specs*). Let's listen to how they reacted to their new glasses.

Discussion Questions

Significant Details:

What happened to Ronald Morgan that made you think he might have needed glasses? (He slid into a girl on the playground, mixed up feed for fish and gerbil, was hit by a ball in gym, had difficulty reading a report, and had difficulty cutting out a snowflake.)

How did Ronald behave when he went to the eye doctor? (He was excited about glasses; in fact, he thought they would help him become superior in everything.)

Main Ideas:

What happened when Ronald wore his new glasses to school? (He became discouraged because he still couldn't do everything perfectly.)

How did Ronald finally adjust to his new glasses? (Teacher sent him a note explaining what to expect and not expect from glasses; then he was finally able to cut and draw better.)

Questions Comparing and Contrasting the Stories

Significant Details:

Ronald and Arthur both had a grown-up who helped them adjust to wearing glasses. Who helped them? (Their teachers.) How were they helpful? (Miss Tyler helped Ronald realize that glasses are not a miracle cure, and Arthur's teacher helped him realize that glasses are not unattractive.)

Personal Judgment:

When children have problems, who do you think offers the most help and comfort, other children or adults? Why do you think that?

Personal Prophecy:

Imagine you are either Iris, Arthur, or Ronald. How would you have reacted to getting new glasses?

*See *Arthur's Eyes*, page 16, and *Spectacles*, page 175. (*Note:* All three stories deal with children getting new glasses. Any of the three stories could be used alone, though the three blend together well to cover this topic.)

Watch the Stars Come Out

AUTHOR: Rikki Levinson

ILLUSTRATOR: Diane Goode

PUBLISHING INFORMATION:
Dutton, 1985, HB, ISBN 0-525-44205-7
Macmillan (Reading Rainbow), 1987, PB,
ISBN 0-02-688766-5

SUGGESTED AGES: 7–9

TOPICS: Families
Immigrants

THEME: Emigrating to America was an exciting,
though often miserable, experience.

Setting the Stage

Between 1820 and 1920 about thirty-five million
people came to our country to live. They were
called *immigrants*. To become American citizens,
they had to learn to speak the English language,
obey the laws, and pass a test about this country.

Most immigrants came on ships across the Atlantic Ocean. After 1886, as the ships entered New
York Harbor, they sailed by the colossal Statue of
Liberty, which became a symbol of the new life in
America for the immigrants. The ships then landed
at Ellis Island. Officials filled out information for
each person, sometimes changing names to make
them easier to spell and pronounce. Today, Ellis
Island is a museum where the old records of immigrants remain. Many people have looked at them
to find out about their ancestors.

Bridge

The cover of our story shows immigrants getting
ready to board a ship for America. How do you
suppose the little boy and girl feel about their upcoming journey? Let's learn more about these immigrants
in Rikki Levinson's *Watch the Stars Come Out*.

Discussion Questions

Logical Discussion:
Grandma's Mama would have been the little girl's
what? (Great grandmother.)

What different problems made the voyage so
difficult for people? (There were many old people
and small children and babies; people suffered
from seasickness, poor food, uncomfortable sleep-
ing arrangements, cold, a long journey, and poverty.)

Significant Detail:
What did the little girl take with her to provide
security? (Her doll.)

Personal Prophecy:
If you were to take a scary trip without a parent,
what would you take along?

Logical Deductions:
Why do you think doctors gave the children med-
ical exams? (To detect any serious health problems
or diseases.)

Some sisters and brothers fight with one another.
Do you think those children fought with one an-
other on the trip? (No.) Why do you think that way?
(They had only one another.)

Personal Relevance:
Has there ever been a time when you had to
depend on a sister or brother? What happened?

Logical Deductions:
Mama thought their apartment was a "palace."
What does that tell you about their reasons for
emigrating? (They must have felt they would be
better off economically in America.)

How do you think the children felt to be freshly
bathed, shampooed, fed, and close to their mother
and father once again? (Relieved, happy, wonderful.)

Personal Judgment:
Who do you think may have worried more: the
mother and father, who knew how long and difficult the journey was and how young and inexpe-
rienced their children were; or the children, who

were traveling with strangers to a strange land with no parent to assist them? Why do you feel that way?

Activities

Poetry:
Here are the words of the famous poem by Emma Lazarus that is on the base of the Statue of Liberty.

> Give me your tired, your poor,
> Your huddled masses yearning to breathe free,
> The wretched refuse of your teeming shores.
> Send these, the homeless, tempest-tost, to me,
> I lift my lamp beside the golden door.

A discussion of the meaning of the poem and its feasibility in today's world would be an interesting activity with nine-year-olds and older.

Writing:
Ask children if their parents or grandparents tell them stories about "the old days." Do they enjoy listening to these stories? Have them tell or write down stories that they will want to tell their children and grandchildren.

Creative Thinking:
For a creative thinking activity, ask children how the brother kept track of time. (He notched a stick.) Have them pretend that they are in a similar situation. They need to invent a way to keep track of time without using a calendar. They may take some *reasonable* materials with them.

Craft:
Younger children can make the cut-and-color Statue of Liberty. See Activity 76.

Research:
This story could pique interest in Ellis Island, the Statue of Liberty, and citizenship requirements. Brainstorm interesting questions and use the media center to help children discover facts about our immigrant heritage.

Writing:
Children could keep journals for the two immigrant children for the four weeks. They would need to study the pictures from the book for ideas, especially for the third week. The first and last weeks have many ideas. This project could help children identify with the many immigrant children who started their life in America this way.

From *After the Story's Over: Your Enrichment Guide to 88 Read-Aloud Children's Classics,* published by Scott, Foresman and Company. Copyright © 1991 Linda K. Garrity.

Directions:

Make your own Statue of Liberty. Color it light blue-green. Cut out and glue onto tagboard. Cut around statue and cut out extra base piece. Insert base piece in slit to stand up.

When I Was Young in the Mountains

AUTHOR: Cynthia Rylant

ILLUSTRATOR: Diane Goode

PUBLISHING INFORMATION:
Dutton, 1982, HB, ISBN 0-525-42525-X
Dutton, 1985, PB, ISBN 0-525-44198-0

SUGGESTED AGES: 6–9

TOPICS: Families
Grandfathers
Grandmothers

THEME: A loving family, rather than riches, makes one happy.

Setting the Stage

What do you think is important or necessary for a child to be happy?

Bridge

The children in this story by Cynthia Rylant do not seem to have a mother or a father, nice clothes, toys, or a lovely home. Yet they are happy children. I wonder why. Let's find out more about them as the little girl explains their life in *When I Was Young in the Mountains*.

Discussion Questions

Logical Deductions:
The children in the story lived with their grandparents, rather than their parents. The book does not explain why. What would your guesses be? (The parents might be away or they might be dead.)

What mountains did the children live in? (The Appalachian Mountains. This is one of those questions that the adult will ask and then probably answer, showing children on a map where the Appalachian Mountains are located. The adult could also point out the context clues: coal-mining, low mountains with too much foliage for Rockies.)

Significant Detail:
What did the children have for dinner? (Hot corn bread, pinto beans, and fried okra.)

Personal Relevance:
Have you ever eaten any of those foods? Have you ever eaten all three of them together for a meal?

Do you go swimming in the summertime?

Personal Prophecy:
Would you have enjoyed swimming in the muddy swimming hole with the snakes?

Logical Deduction:
Look at the picture of the grocery store. Do you think this story happened in recent times or a long time ago? (Long ago.) What makes you think that? (Everything is old-fashioned looking.)

Personal Prophecy:
Would you have enjoyed buying groceries long ago? What might have been some disadvantages (problems)?

Would you have posed for your picture with the dead snake?

Main Idea:
Their life was so different from yours. Why were the children so happy and contented? (They were loved and cared for by their grandparents, and they loved the Appalachian area.)

Activities

Art:
Children could paint an illustration of a favorite scene from the story. Before beginning to paint, they need to consider the background and the size of the buildings and people that they want to include. It's sometimes helpful for children to lightly sketch in the foreground before they dip into paint.

Cooking:
Making homemade cornbread and butter would be a good activity for this story. The recipes are found on page 146.

From *After the Story's Over: Your Enrichment Guide to 88 Read-Aloud Children's Classics*, published by Scott, Foresman and Company. Copyright © 1991 Linda K. Garrity.

Where the Wild Things Are

AUTHOR: Maurice Sendak

ILLUSTRATOR: Maurice Sendak

PUBLISHING INFORMATION:
Harper & Row, 1963, HB, ISBN 0-06-025520-X
Harper & Row, 1963, LB, ISBN 0-06-025521-8
Harper Trophy, 1984, PB, ISBN 0-06-443055-3

SUGGESTED AGES: 5–6

TOPIC: Imagination

THEME: Children enjoy imagining situations where they are all-powerful.

Setting the Stage

Do you ever like to imagine magical places where you are the boss and exciting things happen all the time? Tell about your favorite "pretend" play. Pretending is one of the best parts of being a child because you can be and do anything you've ever wished. Grown-ups don't usually act out their pretend games, but they enjoy thinking about them.

Bridge

Look at the cover of today's book. Do you think this is a real or imaginary place? What makes you think that? Let's listen to Maurice Sendak's *Where the Wild Things Are* to find out who imagined such a place and what happened there.

Discussion Questions

Logical Deduction:
Why do you think Max was so naughty that evening? (He wore his wolf suit.)

Significant Detail:
What was Max's punishment? (He was sent to his room without supper.)

Logical Deduction:
Why do you think Max went to a place where there were all sorts of wild things? (His mother called him a "wild thing," which might have given him the idea.)

Significant Detail:
How did Max tame the wild things? (He stared into their yellow eyes without blinking once.)

Main Idea:
Why do you think Max wanted to be the boss of the wild things? (Because in real life his mother was the boss.)

Logical Deduction:
Why do you think Max wanted to have a "wild rumpus" with the wild things? (Maybe because his mother wouldn't allow it, or he liked lively play.)

Personal Prophecy:
If you had been Max and you had gone to a strange and different land, what sort of creatures would you have wanted to be with?

Significant Detail:
When Max wanted to end the wild rumpus, what did he do? (He told the wild things to stop and then sent them to bed without supper.)

Logical Deduction:
Why do you suppose he did that? (That was how his mother stopped him from being wild.)

Personal Judgment:
Which do you think is more true: we treat others the way we would like to be treated; or we treat others the way we are treated?

Significant Detail:
Why did Max want to leave the "wild things"? (He was lonely and hungry.)

Logical Deduction:
Why do you think Max's mother gave him his supper after all? (She may have thought he had learned his lesson or been punished enough.)

Personal Judgments:

Do you think Max's mother loves him? Why do you think so?

Do you think Max's mother punished him because she disliked him or because she loved him? Explain why you think so.

Activities

Drama:

This story lends itself to a puppet show, using stick puppets. Children can use their creativity to develop their own "wild things" puppets. See Activity 77.

Craft:

Have children lie down in a variety of positions on large sheets of butcher paper. Quickly trace around their bodies with a black crayon. Then have them use paint, crayons, or markers to fill in the "wild things." Emphasize the "terrible eyes, claws, and teeth." Cut the figures out and staple on walls for a unique display of Sendak's classic.

Cooking:

Making deviled eggs is a great activity for young fingers. Vinegar adds the pizazz but can be eliminated for a milder version. Paper cups can also be used in place of bowls for quick clean-up.

MAX'S BOATS

1. Boil an egg for five minutes. Drain and cool.
2. Peel the egg.
3. Cut in half.
4. Pop out the yolks carefully and place in a small bowl.
5. Crumble up the yolks with a fork.
6. Add and stir together:
   2 teaspoons mayonnaise
   1/4 teaspoon sugar
   a sprinkle salt
   1/8 teaspoon vinegar
7. Scoop the yolk mixture into the egg halves.
8. Make two sails with your name on them, using toothpicks and scotchtape.
9. Stick them in your boats and refrigerate.

Directions:

Draw and color Max and his boat. Cut around the outside edge of both. Glue tongue depressor or ice cream stick on back. Make your own "wild things" puppets and create a new adventure for Max.

The Whingdingdilly

AUTHOR: Bill Peet

ILLUSTRATOR: Bill Peet

PUBLISHING INFORMATION:
Houghton Mifflin, 1970, LB, ISBN 0-395-24729-2
Houghton Mifflin, 1982, PB, ISBN 0-395-31381-3

SUGGESTED AGES: 6–8

TOPICS: Pets
Self-concept

THEME: Be yourself.

Setting the Stage

Have you ever wished that you could be someone famous, like a sports figure or rock star or television star? Who would you like to be?

Bridge

In today's story by Bill Peet we meet Scamp, a loveable but foolish dog, who wished he could be someone different. Let's see what happened to Scamp's wish in *The Whingdingdilly*.

Discussion Questions

Significant Detail:
What embarrassing event caused Scamp to run away? (Orvie laughed at him for imitating Palomar.)

Personal Relevance:
Have you ever been embarrassed by someone catching you daydreaming or pretending when you were unaware? What did you do?

Significant Detail:
What animal parts were used in the Whingdingdilly? Look at the picture to help you. (A camel's hump, a giraffe's neck, a zebra's hind legs and tail, an elephant's front legs and ears, a reindeer's antlers, and a rhinoceros's nose.)

Main Idea:
Was being famous as wonderful as Scamp had thought it would be? (No.) Why not? (People poked and pulled and stared at him, and he was no longer free and loved for himself.)

Personal Judgments:
Often famous people can't go out to eat or shopping or go places with their families without people mobbing them. Do you think the public should ignore famous people so they can lead normal lives, or do you think famous people should expect to sign autographs and visit with fans each time they go out as a price for their fame and fortune?

A curse is a bad wish given to someone. An ancient Chinese curse reads, "May all your dreams or wishes come true." Why would that be a curse rather than a good wish?

Main Idea:
Do you think that Scamp will be jealous of Palomar in the future? (No.) Why not? (He learned his lesson.)

Activity

Craft:
Making a flip book can be fun for children. Perhaps some will be inspired to try their hand at it. They have to be careful to keep the dimensions of the animals at the edges of the pages identical. See Activity 78.

Directions:

Color the cover and the animals. Cut out pieces on dotted lines. Staple sections together in order under the cover page where indicated by ├───┤. Use paperclips to hold pieces together while stapling. Flip up pages to make new animals.

William's Doll

AUTHOR: Charlotte Zolotow

ILLUSTRATOR: William Pène DuBois

PUBLISHING INFORMATION:
Harper & Row, 1972, HB, ISBN 0-06-027047-0
Harper & Row, 1972, LB, ISBN 0-06-027048-9
Harper Trophy, 1985, PB, ISBN 0-06-443067-7

SUGGESTED AGES: 5–6

TOPICS: Self-concept
Toys

THEME: Children's playthings should not be limited by sexist notions.

Setting the Stage

What are your favorite toys?

Bridge

Today's story is about a boy named William who wanted a special toy. His father bought him lots of wonderful toys, but not the one thing that William really wanted. Let's read our story to find out what William wanted and see if he got it.

Discussion Questions

Significant Detail:
What did William want most of all? (A doll.)

Logical Deduction:
Why didn't his father and brother want him to have one? (They thought it would make him a sissy.)

Significant Detail:
Who thought that William *should* have a doll? (His grandmother.)

Main Idea:
Why did she think it would be a good idea? (She thought he should play with a doll so he could practice fathering.)

Personal Prophecy:
If you were William's father, would you give him a doll? Why do you feel that way?

Personal Judgments:
Do you think it is all right for girls to play with cars and trucks and footballs?

Do you think it is all right for boys to play with dolls and playhouses?

Activities

Supplementary Material:
There is a section about *William's Doll* in the book and film *Free to Be You and Me* that would coordinate well.

Craft:
Children can create their own super toy store in a small box by making counters and signs and stocking it with tiny trinkets.

Interview:
Six-year-olds might enjoy interviewing their parents about the differences in role expectations between today's children and the last generation's children. Such issues as girls in sports, girls wearing slacks to school, and boys as babysitters could be discussed.

The Wump World

AUTHOR: Bill Peet

ILLUSTRATOR: Bill Peet

PUBLISHING INFORMATION:
Houghton Mifflin, 1970, HB, ISBN 0-395-19841-0
Houghton Mifflin, 1981, PB, ISBN 0-395-19841-0

SUGGESTED AGES: 5–9

TOPIC: Environment

THEME: Total disregard of the environment results in a world unfit for habitation.

Setting the Stage

What is pollution? What do you think causes air pollution? . . . water pollution? . . . destruction of wildlife and natural parks?

Bridge

Bill Peet tells us a story about an imaginary world called Wump World where there is no pollution. I wonder what this imaginary world would be like? With Bill Peet as the illustrator, the book will probably have some very interesting-looking creatures. Let's listen to discover what Wump World is like and what happens to it.

Discussion Questions

Personal Judgment:
Which statement do you agree with more: since no one apparently lived in Wump World, it was only reasonable to go ahead and lay claim to it; or, it's not right to march in and take over a land without making sure it doesn't belong to someone else.

Personal Prophecy:
If you had been the world chief, how would you have planned and designed the new settlement for the Pollutians?

Main Idea:
Why did the Pollutians leave Wump World rather than try to improve it? (It was so badly ruined that it was easier to start over.)

Personal Relevance:
What are all the things you can do to help prevent pollution (including litter) in your world?

Activities

Creative Thinking/Drawing:
Show children the second page of the story. Point out the trees. What are they called? (Bumbershoot trees.) Bumbershoots are what British people call umbrellas. Do you see the resemblance? Have children create their own special trees and shrubs on paper and then title them.

Craft:
Children can help the Wumps find their way back to their home by the bumbershoots in the maze activity. See Activity 79.

Directions:

Draw the Wumps at the bottom of the maze. Then help the Wumps find their way out of the caverns and back up to the grassy meadows.

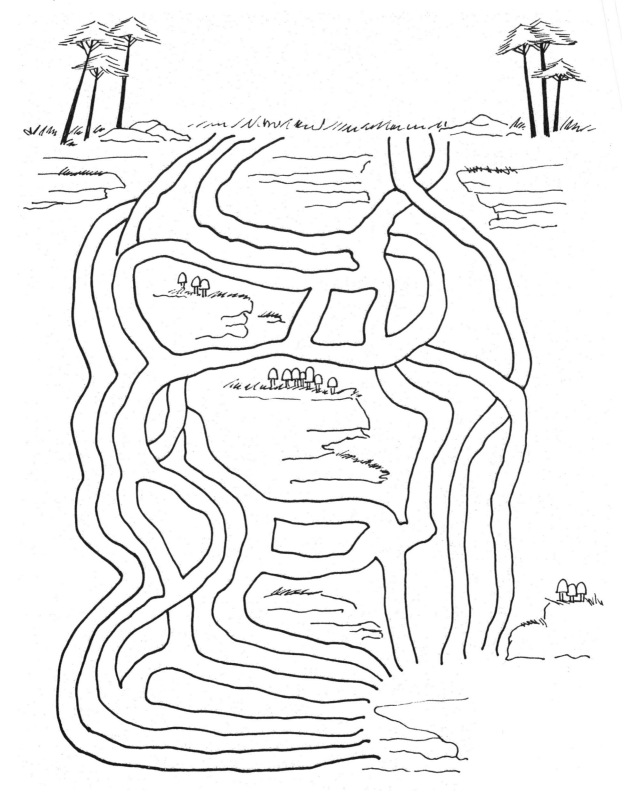

Author, Title, and Topic Index

Alexander and the Terrible, Horrible, No Good, Very
    Bad Day   6, 7, 8, 9
Allard, Harry
    Miss Nelson Is Missing!   124
Amos and Boris   10, 11, 12
ANIMALS
    Annie and the Wild Animals   13, 14, 15
    Jumanji   102, 103, 104
Annie and the Wild Animals   13, 14, 15
Arthur's Eyes   16, 17
Arthur's Halloween   18, 19
Arthur's Tooth   20, 21, 22
Arthur's Valentine   23, 24, 25

Baby Sister for Frances, A   26, 27, 28
BABYSITTERS
    Jerome the Babysitter   98, 99, 100, 101
Bah! Humbug?   29, 30
Balian, Lorna
    Bah! Humbug?   29, 30
    Humbug Rabbit   87, 88, 89
    Leprechauns Never Lie   108, 109, 110
    Sometimes It's Turkey—Sometimes It's
        Feathers   172, 173, 174
    Sweet Touch, The   178, 179, 180
Barrett, Judi
    Cloudy with a Chance of Meatballs   45, 46
Bate, Lucy
    Little Rabbit's Loose Tooth   116, 117
BEDTIME
    Bedtime for Frances   31, 32
Bedtime for Frances   31, 32
Bemelmans, Ludwig
    Madeline   121, 122, 123
Berenstain, Stan and Jan
    Berenstain Bears Go to School, The   33, 34
Berenstain Bears Go to School, The   33, 34
Best Friends   35, 36
Biggest House in the World, The   37, 38
Birthday for Frances, A   39, 40
BIRTHDAYS
    Birthday for Frances, A   39, 40
Blume, Judy
    Pain and the Great One, The   149, 150, 151
    Bread and Jam for Frances   41, 42
Brett, Jan
    Annie and the Wild Animals   13, 14, 15
Brown, Marc
    Arthur's Eyes   16, 17
    Arthur's Halloween   18, 19

Arthur's Tooth   20, 21, 22
Arthur's Valentine   23, 24, 25
Brown, Margaret Wise
    Runaway Bunny, The   170, 171
Burton, Virginia Lee
    Little House, The   113, 114, 115

CANDY
    Arthur's Valentine   23, 24, 25
    Harriet's Halloween Candy   75, 76
    Sweet Touch, The   178, 179, 180
Carlson, Nancy
    Harriet's Halloween Candy   75, 76
Carrick, Carol
    Old Mother Witch   143, 144
    Patrick's Dinosaurs   153, 154, 155
    Rabbit for Easter, A   167, 168, 169
Chair for My Mother, A   43, 44
CHAIRS
    Chair for My Mother, A   43, 44
    Peter's Chair   156, 157
CHANUKAH
    There's No Such Thing as a Chanukah Bush, Sandy
        Goldstein   195, 196, 197, 198
Christelow, Eileen
    Jerome the Babysitter   98, 99, 100, 101
CHRISTMAS
    Bah! Humbug?   29, 30
    Cobweb Christmas   47, 48
    Polar Express, The   160, 161
    Star Mother's Youngest Child   176, 177
    There's No Such Thing as a Chanukah Bush, Sandy
        Goldstein   195, 196, 197, 198
Climo, Shirley
    Cobweb Christmas, The   47, 48
Cloudy With a Chance of Meatballs   45, 46
Cobweb Christmas, The   47, 48
Cohen, Barbara
    Molly's Pilgrim   128, 129, 130, 131
Cole, Babette
    Trouble with Mom, The   202, 203, 204
Cooney, Barbara
    Miss Rumphius   125, 126, 127
Corduroy   49, 50
Country Bunny and the Little Gold Shoes, The   51,
    52, 53
Cranberry Thanksgiving   54, 55
CROCODILES/ALLIGATORS
    House on East 88th Street, The   82, 83
    Jerome the Babysitter   98, 99, 100, 101

From *After the Story's Over: Your Enrichment Guide to 88 Read-Aloud Children's Classics*, published by Scott, Foresman and Company. Copyright © 1991 Linda K. Garrity.

From *After the Story's Over: Your Enrichment Guide to 88 Read-Aloud Children's Classics,* published by Scott, Foresman and Company. Copyright © 1991 Linda K. Garrity.

From *After the Story's Over: Your Enrichment Guide to 88 Read-Aloud Children's Classics,* published by Scott, Foresman and Company. Copyright © 1991 Linda K. Garrity.

Author, Title, and Topic Index

From *After the Story's Over: Your Enrichment Guide to 88 Read-Aloud Children's Classics,* published by Scott, Foresman and Company. Copyright © 1991 Linda K. Garrity.